T0096337

GAME OVER

THE GAMES WE LOVED TO PLAY AND THE CONSOLES TIME FORGOT

CONTENTS

WELCOME TO GAME OVER!

THE year 2018 marks the 40th anniversary of *Space Invaders*. It is hard to believe how far games have come in such a relatively short amount of time. It took cinema over 30 years to add sound, and a good few years after that to start using colour. In comparison, games have gone from simple monochrome blocks to high-definition real-time 3D worlds within our own lifetime.

That, of course, assumes that you, dear reader, are one of the many children of the 1970s and 1980s, now staring down the barrel of middle age and wondering why your knees make a loud clicking noise when you sit down. For those of us who grew up with gaming, consider this book a chance to relive the experience, year by year, from those earliest arcade memories to the dawn of the modern console era at the end of the 20th century.

If you're not one of those oldsters, then strap yourself in for a blast through gaming history from the pixel-driven Stone Age to, well, whatever the gaming equivalent of the 1940s is. Basically, if you love games today, this is how we got here.

As with any great story worth telling, there will be highs and lows along the way. You will come face to face with games you loved, and games you've tried to forget. You'll bear witness to the birth of giants, and the hilarious demise of absolute cack.

It's a dizzying journey, with a lot to take in, and while the title may sound worryingly final, don't panic. It may be game over for one era of gaming, but as every player knows...you can always start over.

WARNING!

Some of the things in this book may make you realise that you are now very old, and that might make you feel sad. If this happens, just sit in a warm bath and listen to the theme tune from *The Fall Guy* until it passes.

THE DAWN OF GAMING

Today's gamers have no idea what the disco generation had
to go through in order to get our gaming fix...

PEOPLE have been competing against computers since the 1950s, when boffins would spend their free time playing Tic Tac Toe against wheezing room-sized machines, using punch cards and lightbulbs to follow the action. Look, it was only a few years after the war. Everything was in ruins and you couldn't buy bananas anywhere. Any entertainment was a bonus.

Everything changed in 1961. That was when American college workers Martin Graetz, Steve Russell and Wayne Wiitanen wrote *Spacewar*, the world's first multiplayer shoot-em-up that was played in real time, on a real screen. OK, so it was really just two tiny rocket ships floating around a black hole, firing single pixel dots at each other, but when the alternative was playing noughts and crosses against a giant vacuum cleaner, it was clear that a world-changing technology was upon us.

The idea of "computer games" wouldn't properly reach the public consciousness for another 17 years, however. It took that long for companies to seize on the potential of electronic amusements, and find a form that could rake in the cash. And that form was the mighty arcade machine.

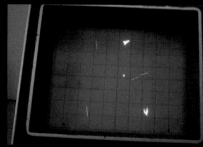

6

Oh, the arcade. It's all very convenient for today's young gamers, with millions of new titles ready to slither down the data pipes into their phones and consoles without ever leaving the couch, but back in gaming's prehistoric age if you wanted to play a game you had to go and find them. And that meant venturing into the noisy smoke-filled dungeon of the local arcade.

Usually found quietly rotting on the promenade of tourist trap seaside towns, or hanging off the back of the local fleapit cinema, the original arcades were genuinely terrifying places. With sticky carpets, musty smells and a clientele that looked like the cast of last night's *Crimewatch* reconstruction, entry into these migraine portals was a true rite of passage for 1970s youth.

Dozens of cabinets all shrieked and flashed for your attention simultaneously, with gaudy visuals painted on the sides like second hand wardrobes disguised as prog rock albums. This was where you could fritter away your bus fare home, 10p at a time, in pursuit of the greatest victory of all: the chance to enter the three-letter swear word of your choice into the high score table, for the whole town to see!

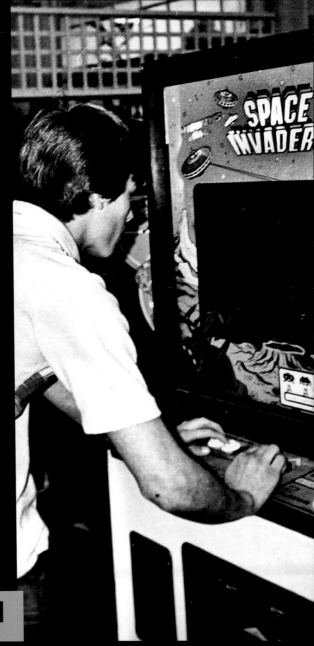

Released in 1978

SPACE INVADERS

They're coming!

Aliens attack the Earth in suspiciously neat rows, and spark a revolution.

FOR many people, their first encounter with gaming will have come from seeing *Space Invaders* in the corner of a pub or chip shop. The first truly mass-market gaming blockbuster, Taito's *Space Invaders* was a cultural phenomenon that caught the imagination of a public that had been turned on to science fiction by *Star Wars* the year before.

You know how it goes, of course. Everybody does. Rows of aliens descend from above and you must shoot them down before they reach the bottom of the screen. There was no way to win at *Space Invaders*. Each screen cleared simply started over again, and the game's increasing speed came from the player whittling down the enemies allowing the code to run faster and faster.

The image of the *Space Invaders* alien is still associated with gaming, even to people who have never held a joypad, and the game itself has inspired everything from novelty disco records to endless TV and movie parodies.

It's the sounds that are burned into most player's minds though. That ominous bom-bom-bom-bom soundtrack, like a brass band farting in unison, is the gaming equivalent of the famous Jaws theme and can still loosen the bowels of older gamers even now.

Yawn... With no way to actually beat the game, *Space Invaders* was frustratingly annoying!

PAC-MAN

Pill-munching, ghost-gobbling pizza creature captivates the world!

WHILE *Space Invaders* gave gaming its first mainstream hit, it wasn't until 1980 that games got their first global mascot: *Pac-Man*!

Creator Toru Iwatani was famously inspired by a pizza with a slice missing when designing his circular yellow hero. Iwatani also deliberately made the game cute in order to appeal to girls, as well as the teen boys who were already becoming gaming's core audience. Political correctness had yet to reach Japan, you see.

That's not to say *Pac-Man* was easy. It's actually incredibly hard, with each of the four ghosts chasing you around the dot-filled maze following a unique (if basic) artificial intelligence. The red ghost chases behind you, while the pink will try to get in front. The blue and orange ghosts flip their behaviour randomly, sometimes chasing, sometimes running away, to keep you on your toes.

The funniest thing about *Pac-Man* is the origin of his name. Originally called *Puck Man*, because of his shape, the title was hurriedly altered once western arcade owners found customers vandalising the first letter on the cabinet so it said something rather different…

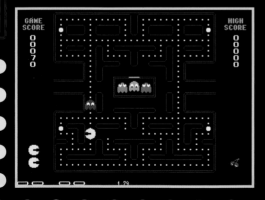

Pac-Man is featured in the New York Museum of Modern Art!

Released in: **1980**

BEWARE THE KILL SCREEN

The ultimate game over for hardcore players!

TODAY'S games are made to be beaten. Nobody buys the new *Call of Duty* wondering if they'll get to the end. Of course you will. They spent millions of dollars on it. The only reason people don't reach the end of a modern game is because they get bored.

There was no such hand-holding for arcade gamers in the 1980s. This was the era of rock hard difficulty and repetitive gameplay, where bragging rights didn't come from how many digital trophies you were handed for taking part, but for how long you could survive with your mates crowded round, egging you on.

As a result, most of gaming's earliest hits had no ending. Or at least, none that ended on purpose. This is where the fabled kill screen came in. These were the garbled screens that appeared when the game could go no further and simply crashed. Reaching a kill screen was the ultimate achievement, the sign that you were not only good at a game, but so good that the game itself couldn't keep up.

Famous kill screens include *Donkey Kong*, which breaks on the 117th screen by giving the player only seven seconds to beat it, and Nintendo's *Duck Hunt*, which flies to pieces if you get to level 100. Both *Pac-Man* and *Dig Dug* break down once you hit level 256. Today, the problem would probably be solved with a downloadable patch, and a piece of gaming history would be gone forever.

what just happened?

The most common cause of a kill screen is an integer overflow. Do you want to know what that is? Be warned: it does involve a bit of maths. Basically, an integer is a whole number stored by the game's code – such as what level the player is on. Thanks to the limited storage of early computer hardware, there were limits to how many integers could be stored. Go past that limit and the code can't cope with the information and crashes to a halt. Just like your mum trying to set up email on her phone.

pac-attack!

Pac-Man's "256" glitch is so famous that it was used as the basis for a 35th anniversary game in 2015, from the makers of *Crossy Road*. Players must keep navigating an endless vertical maze, staying ahead of the glitch which chases after you from the bottom of the screen.

THE AGE OF ATARI

Gaming comes home in chunky style!

IF you wanted to play arcade games at home in the late 1970s, there was really only one choice: the Atari VCS. This American "video computer system" boasted thick clacking levers, a stiff one-button joystick and a stylish wooden veneer on the front. Yes, this was the only gaming console that matched your Nan's cocktail cabinet.

Atari games came on sturdy plastic bricks which slotted into the port on the top of the machine. That's quite appropriate, given that games for the Atari 2600 had graphics that looked like they were made from Duplo, with enormous chunky pixels and a limited colour palette. When mum and dad said gaming would give you square eyes, they were closer to the truth than they knew.

Ready Jedi Go!

Atari came along at just the right time to catch the wave of *Star Wars* mania, and was home to the first ever *Star Wars* console games. Check out this super chunky scene from *The Empire Strikes Back*!

King of the Swingers!

One of the 2600's biggest hits was *Pitfall*, an *Indiana Jones* style jungle adventure which stayed at the top of the Billboard sales chart for an entire year!

When the Atari VCS first launched in America, on 11 September 1977, it cost $199. In today's money, that's equivalent to almost $800. Eager gamers, wide-eyed at the opportunity to play both arcade hits and original new games in their living room, weren't put off by the price. Atari went on to introduce the more powerful 5200 model and in 1982 renamed the original as the Atari 2600. It eventually sold over 30 million consoles, making it one of the most successful pieces of gaming hardware of all time!

For Play or Foreplay?

Since games companies weren't sure who was buying these new gaming machines, it led to some unusual tie-in games being released. For instance, 20th Century Fox thought a game based on raunchy 1982 sex comedy *Porky's* would be a hit!

Quids In!

The most valuable Atari 2600 game ever released is *Air Raid*. Launched in limited numbers in 1982, and recognisable for its weird blue-handled cartridge, only a handful of boxed copies still exist and often sell for more than £20,000 at auction. Check the loft!

13

E.T. COMES HOME...

©1982 ATARI

9924

And ends up buried
in the desert.

ATARI 2600

E.T. THE EXTRA-TERRESTRIAL™

ONE of the biggest movies of 1982 was, of course, Steven Spielberg's sci-fi weepie *E.T. the Extra Terrestrial*. Spinning the touching yarn of a lonely young boy and his magical new pal from outer space, the film seized the public by the heartstrings and became one of the defining pop culture moments of the decade.

A video game was clearly required. Luckily, Spielberg was a hip young dude and he loved video games. A deal was quickly struck to turn his blockbuster smash into an Atari 2600 game in time for Christmas. The man given the job was Howard Scott Warshaw, whose shoot-em-up *Yar's Revenge* had been a cult hit on the console.

Trouble was, Warshaw started work at the end of July. The game had to be ready by the start of September in order to be produced and delivered to shops for Christmas. Yes, this blockbuster game that Atari reportedly paid over $20m for, had to be churned out by one guy in about five weeks!

The E.T. game has since become known as "the worst game of all time", but that's a bit unfair. It's not very good, but there were – and are – plenty that are worse. The player guides a lumpy E.T. sprite around scenes from the movie, looking for the three pieces of his home-made spacephone that have been lost in a series of pits. Reese's Pieces candy tops up his health, which is drained by, well, by doing anything. Even just moving saps his lifeforce. No wonder he's so wrinkly.

It's a noble attempt at translating the heartfelt drama of Spielberg's movie to an interactive form, but the game was too simple, too boring and too frustrating for young gamers. Unfortunately, Atari had already produced millions of cartridges, so when sales began to dry up thanks to poor word of mouth, it was stuck with warehouses full of stock that it just couldn't shift.

Many cartridges ended up being buried in a landfill in New Mexico, a fact that was considered by many to be urban myth until filmmaker Zak Penn (*X-Men 2*, *Hulk*) dug them up for his *Atari: Game Over* documentary in 2014.

It wasn't really E.T.'s fault. Atari had over-produced too many low quality games, flooding the US market and driving away its own customers. By 1984, Atari was going out of business and by 1985 its arcade division was sold to Namco in Japan, while its home console business was bought by Commodore. It kept the Atari name, though, which still lives on today.

MANIC MINER

Released in:
1983

Descend into the depths with a rock hard classic!

IF there was one Spectrum game that literally everybody owned, it was *Manic Miner*. Created by 17-year-old Matthew Smith, the game put players in control of Miner Willy, an amusingly named entrepreneurial go-getter who decides to get rich by exploring the vast and frankly surreal caves beneath his house.

Most players, of course, struggled to get past the first of the game's screens. Even at a time when most games were notoriously tough, it doesn't take long to burn through your extra lives in *Manic Miner*. Every leap must be made with pixel precision, and literally everything kills you. Even tiny green plants. Maybe Willy just had really, really bad hayfever.

Each screen was also played against the clock, as Willy's air slowly ran out. Despite this rather urgent deadline, he never managed to move much faster than a casual stroll, and his slow motion leaps were surprisingly chilled out considering the constant mortal peril he was facing.

Of course, in keeping with the game design style of the era, once you manage to beat all twenty screens, the game simply starts over again without even so much as a congratulations. Thanks for that...

Among the enemies Miner Willy faces during his adventure are Ewok teddy bears, copyright-baiting Pac-Men, the infamous "Kong Beast," and carnivorous toilets!

JET SET WILLY

Released in: **1984**

Willy's back…and this time he's loaded!

IN the sequel to *Manic Miner*, Willy is now incredibly rich thanks to his mining exploits, and lives in a gigantic mansion. Unfortunately, this being a 1980s platform game, the mansion is full of deadly platforms and bizarre creatures mindlessly roaming backwards and forwards. After a particularly hardcore party, Willy's fearsome housekeeper Maria won't let him go to bed until he tidies the whole house. Hey, who's the boss around here anyway?

A spin-off game called *The Perils of Willy* was released for the Vic 20 the same year, and a remixed *Jet Set Willy* remake followed in 1985, but that was it as far as Miner Willy's official gaming career was concerned. A final game – to be called *Miner Willy Meets the Taxman* – was never completed or released. But then, it was the 1980s. Trouble with miners was very much the in-thing back then…

Jet Set Willy couldn't actually be completed when it first launched, thanks to a series of glitches known to fans as 'the Attic Bug'. Entering the attic room on the map corrupted game data, meaning other rooms would kill Willy as soon as he entered. Cheekily, the publisher tried to pretend this was deliberate and the rooms were full of poison gas!

THE SINCLAIR REVOLUTION

Sir Clive turns Britain's bedroom gamers into a cottage industry.

WHILE the US games industry was shuddering from the rapid rise and embarrassing fall of Atari, here in the UK the computer scene was in rude health thanks almost entirely to one man: Clive Sinclair.

Balding boffin Clive believed that everybody should be able to tap into the microcomputer revolution, not just big businesses, and he set about launching a range of home computers that could be sold on the high street for affordable prices.

First out of the gate in 1981 was the ZX81, a sort of plastic beermat with touch sensitive alphanumeric pads instead of keys, and a whopping 1 kilobyte of memory. This could be boosted with additional RAM packs which slotted precariously into the back, where the slightest wobble could bring the whole computer to a juddering crash. This is why every ZX81 owner kept a large blob of Blu-Tack handy, to steady their setup and prevent catastrophic data loss.

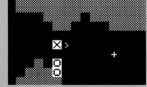

The ZX81 could only construct its graphics from pre-designed blocks, and most of its rudimentary games simply used letters, numbers and punctuation marks that most closely resembled the object in question. Yes, that capital M really was a spaceship, fending off invading ampersands.

Bits and Bytes

Ever wondered what 1k and 16k and 48k meant? Each piece of data – every single letter or number – stored in a computer takes up one bit, and there are eight bits in a byte. The word "computer", for example, needs eight bits – or one byte – to store. So you'd think a kilobyte would be 1000 bytes, right? Wrong. Or at least not back in the 80s, when a kilobyte was actually 1024 bytes, because computer scientists are weird. All that really matters is that the more kilobytes of memory your computer had, the more fun stuff – graphics, sound and so on – a game could cram in!

Do It Yourself!

The ZX81 came in two different versions. Budding electronics whizkids could pay £49 for one in kit form, that had to be assembled at home. If that was too scary, or too much like hard work, a pre-built version could be picked up for £69 instead.

Tape That!

Finding ways to store software in the early days of computing was a real challenge. Atari had used cartridges, but these were expensive to make and couldn't be used to record data at home. Sinclair opted for the humble magnetic tape cassette, which was cheap to source and also meant that WHSmith developed a steady sideline in "data recorders" for gamers to use. In reality, these were usually just imported cassette players so cheap and crackly that they were useless for listening to music!

BATTERIES NOT INCLUDED

No computer? No problem! Wrap your fingers around these gaming gizmos!

WHEN the 1980s saw home computing and game consoles take off in a big way, toy companies like Grandstand, Tomy and Tiger Electronics weren't about to be left behind. Realising there was now a growing market of eager young players who would pounce on anything that even smelled vaguely like a video game, they quickly churned out dozens of relatively simple devices that offered a sort of arcade-like experience, provided you squinted a bit and didn't expect anything too fancy. Here are some of the classics...

Astro Wars

Practically every British bedroom had one of these shoved in the bottom of the wardrobe. Offering a simple riff on arcade shoot-em-ups like *Galaxian*, it used LED bulbs to illuminate the aliens as they "moved" down the screen. With its stubby joystick and comically massive fire button, it was hardly the most exciting game around, but its futuristic shape and silvery sheen made it seem pretty exotic all the same.

Game & Watch

Nintendo wouldn't launch the GameBoy until the end of the 80s, but the Japanese giant kickstarted the handheld gaming boom years before with the arrival of Game & Watch, a series of chocolate-bar-sized games that used LCD screens and limited animation to keep millions of kids quiet during long car journeys. As well as Nintendo hits like *Donkey Kong*, the range also included games based on films, cartoons and comic characters.

Tomytronic 3D

Owning a Tomytronic 3D meant you could shove your face into either a fight for survival against aliens, or it would look like a slow-moving battle against coloured lights, depending on how imaginative you were. It was the same basic tech as Astro Wars, but stuck in what looked like a cross between Luke Skywalker's space binoculars and a knackered old Viewmaster.

As Seen On TV

Loads of blockbuster films and TV shows got their own standalone electronic toy tie-ins, especially if they were science fiction based. *Battlestar Galactica* had a crude Battleships light-up game, *Star Trek* got a similar ship-to-ship combat game, but best of all was *TRON*. Legend had it that if you shoved your face close enough to the crinkled plastic screen, you might get sucked into the game world, just like Jeff Bridges…

THE ZX

Sir Clive tries to teach us about coding

WITH the success of the ZX81, Sir Clive Sinclair quickly moved on to launch an even more powerful home computer. OK, so "more powerful" in 1982 meant 48k of memory rather than 1k, and a handful of colours that went all glitchy if you put them next to each other, but for a generation of British kids it was the dawning of a new age. Except Sinclair wasn't interested in games.

His goal was to simply create an affordable home computer that would teach Britain how to use code and software to improve their lives. Needless to say, while many mums and dads bought one for homework and spreadsheets, it was only a matter of time before the kids took it over for marathon sessions on *Manic Miner*.

The most famous thing about the original 48K Spectrum was that it had rubber keys, an absolutely bizarre decision that still baffles today. Typing anything for a long time on the humble Speccy was like giving a massage to a jellyfish. And not only were the keys soft and spongy, they were covered in multiple functions and phrases from the BASIC programming language, accessible via a frankly terrifying array of shift buttons. Now that the standard PC keyboard is so familiar, the Spectrum looks like some kind of alien artefact, designed to confuse.

The Spectrum didn't even have a dedicated chip for producing sound. All it had was an electronic buzzer that could be made to squawk and fart at different pitches and frequencies. Despite this limitation, cunning computer composers still managed to come up with ways to make this crude noisebox produce actual music, and some Speccy gaming themes are still considered to be chiptune classics today. And that's the ZX Spectrum in a nutshell. It shouldn't have worked. It was a weird design, full of quirks and limitations, but it produced a generation of bedroom enthusiasts who found ingenious ways to make the most of this clunky, brilliant device, and who went on to form the backbone of the British games industry, creating titles like *Tomb Raider* and *Grand Theft Auto*. The Spectrum was an oddball little machine, but it had a massive impact on the world!

SPECTRUM

– and creates a generation of gamers!

The Spectrum wasn't Sir Clive's only 80s invention. He also created a handheld television, a wrist-mounted calculator and, most famously, the C5 electric tricycle…

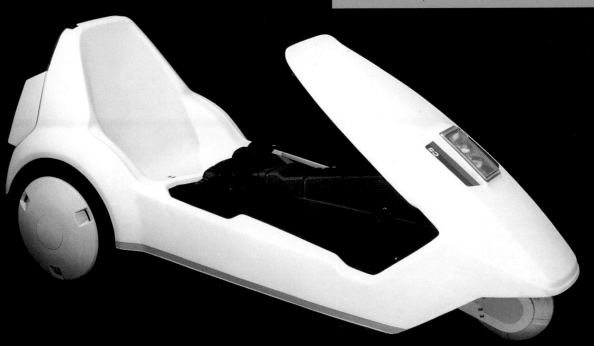

SKOOL DAZE

Players run riot in a miniature version of real school life!

GAMES have always been at their best when they let the player live out some fantastic wish fulfilment, and for kids in the mid-80s what could be more liberating than the idea of breaking every school rule – and getting away with it?

Anarchic classroom sandbox *Skool Daze* puts you in control of Eric, a cheeky schoolboy who must retrieve his inevitably terrible school report from the safe in the headmaster's office. You do this by hitting shields dotted around the school and making them flash, which somehow makes the teachers give you the combination. Look, nobody ever said games should make sense, OK?

The genius of *Skool Daze* was that the school day unfolded around you, with dozens of pixel kids shuffling to different lessons, or to the canteen for lunch. Get spotted by a teacher in the wrong place at the wrong time, and you get given lines as punishment. Get 10,000 lines and you're expelled forever.

You were free to do whatever you wanted, whether that was tormenting the school swot with your catapult or framing the school bully for your own mischief. You could even rename the other characters, including the teachers, to make the game reflect your own real life. Finally, a game that made kids want to stay in school – even if it was just to muck about!

The 1985 sequel, *Back to Skool*, added a water pistol and pet frog to Eric's arsenal, and even had a girl's school next door for even more mayhem!

HORACE GOES SKIING

Terrifying blob creature risks life and limb for winter sports!

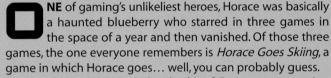

ONE of gaming's unlikeliest heroes, Horace was basically a haunted blueberry who starred in three games in the space of a year and then vanished. Of those three games, the one everyone remembers is *Horace Goes Skiing*, a game in which Horace goes… well, you can probably guess.

Released in:
1982

The game opened with a bit of *Frogger*-esque action as you guided Horace across an often impossibly busy highway in order to rent a pair of skis without being splattered. Manage to do that, and you were rewarded with the chance to slide awkwardly down a mountain, missing flags and hitting trees. At the bottom you had to cross the road – again – before you could have another go.

Horace Goes Skiing was punishingly difficult, but strangely compelling. In the game's most ghoulish feature, you have money instead of lives. If Horace doesn't have enough cash to pay for an ambulance, he's left to die in the gutter. The colours may have been cheery, but the game was pretty dark!

The other games in the series were *Hungry Horace* and *Horace and the Spiders*. Neither was as fun as *Horace Goes Skiing*…

TAPE LOADING ERROR

The pain every 80s gamer dreaded!

WHEN more and more players today download their games direct to their PC, console or smartphone, the idea of games even having a physical form can seem increasingly old-fashioned. But back in the day, when games were recorded on magnetic tape, building the biggest collection of cassettes meant serious playground credibility.

It wasn't the most reliable method of loading data, of course. 1980s games were simple things, and often loaded from the cheapest tape players. It wasn't unusual for different games to require different volume settings in order to successfully load, while the slightest snag, twist or kink in the tape itself could render a beloved game completely unusable. Disaster!

Even if the tape worked, there was still the fact that the data could only be loaded as quickly as the tape allowed. This was certainly not a good

Artificial life simulator *Little Computer People*, for the Spectrum 128k, took over 12 minutes to load! Time for a nap?

time to be impatient, as games could take anywhere from two to five minutes to load – and even then, they could fail and crash right at the end.

Loading a ZX Spectrum game was a particularly nail-biting experience, as not only did you have the constant threat of a tape loading error, but you also had to endure minutes of unholy screeching noises while you waited.

That was the sound of data being played – the same digital shriek made by old dial-up modems – but in the case of a game, that noise would carry on for ages. If you had a Spectrum you'll still remember that sound, burned into your brain after stabbing through your ear drums on a daily basis for years on end. Who could forget the peculiar rhythm it had: BEEEE-DIP BEEEE-DIDDLY-DIP BEEEEEE-DIDDLY DIDDLY…and so on, until your game was loaded, the game crashed or you were kicked off the TV because your dad wanted to watch it.

In the battle to make their games stand out on the shelves, games companies quickly moved on from single cassette cases. Double cases were common, as were increasingly large cardboard boxes – and even thick VHS style plastic cases. All of them, of course, still contained a single tape…

While they were wonky and unreliable, at least you could wind a broken tape back in with a biro. Try doing that with a digital download!

ULTIMATE
PLAY THE GAME

From jetpacks to werewolves, meet the greatest 8-bit developer of all time!

EVERY 1980s computer game collection needed to have at least one game from Ultimate Play the Game. This legendary British code factory, with its metallic blue and green logo, produced a string of hits with very few clunkers, making it one of the most dependable companies around.

In 1983, above their parents' newsagents shop in unsuspecting Ashby-de-la-Zouch, brothers Tim and Chris Stamper made their first million. Ultimate's first game, *Jetpac*, sold over 300,000 copies. Not a bad start!

The company grew rapidly, turning out a stonking seventeen games in just a few years. Ultimate was best known for its isometric "Filmation" games, starting with *Knightlore*, which took the classic platforms and puzzles gameplay of the early 80s and reinvented them in solid three-dimensional worlds.

Ultimate ran out of steam by the late 1980s, but the Stamper boys had already seen where gaming was headed. They were the first UK company to get their hands on the Nintendo Entertainment System and soon began developing console games under a new company called Rare. You know them today as the makers of *Banjo Kazooie*, *GoldenEye* and *Kinect Sports*!

The Ultimate Ultimate Games!

Jetpac

A daft spaceman not only runs out of fuel, but breaks his spaceship into pieces on an alien world. Zip around the screen, put it back together and fill her up with unleaded before blasting off to the next level. A classic!

Atic Atac

Explore a creepy castle, searching for the pieces of the key that will let you escape. Watch out for ghosts and monsters, and use trapdoors and secret passages to get around. An amazingly deep game for 1983!

Sabre Wulf

Guide the sword-waggling Sabreman through a jungle maze on the trail of a magical amulet. Just make sure you don't get trampled by the rhino.

Knightlore

Sabreman goes 3D, and Spectrum gaming is never the same again. Dozens of puzzle-filled rooms, and the chance to turn into a werewolf! What more do you want?

COMMODORE 64

Flashy, colourful
and with actual
proper music –
meet the Spectrum's
glamorous rival!

IN early 1983, only a few months after Sinclair launched its rubber-keyed wonder, the ZX Spectrum, American computer company Commodore released its latest machine as well. The differences couldn't have been more obvious. With a beefy 64k compared to Spectrum's feeble 48k, the Commodore 64 was a veritable sports car of a computer by early 80s standards. Not only did it have a real keyboard, with plastic keys that actually click-clacked when you pressed them rather than just sort of squishing, it also boasted a wider colour palette that didn't dissolve into flickering glitches when more than one colour was used. Even more impressive, the C64 had its own dedicated sound chip – the SID – which meant it could produce more sounds, and more tonally pleasing music, than the Spectrum's humble squawking buzzer.

To put it in movie terms, if the Spectrum was Rocky, an ambitious underdog overcoming adversity in pursuit of a dream, the Commodore was Apollo Creed, a flashy show-boater that could actually back up its glitzy presentation with some real muscle.

****

That these two mismatched machines went on to form gaming's first true brand rivalry is nothing short of amazing. It should have been an easy win for Commodore, but with a wallet-pinching price tag of £399 compared to the Speccy's more generous £175, there were enough cost conscious British parents to ensure that Sinclair's machine could put up a fight where sales were concerned. That fight often took on a literal and physical form in the nation's playgrounds, as youngsters pinned their flag to the mast of whichever machine they owned, and took slurs against their computer very seriously indeed. The SEGA versus Nintendo rivalries that came later were nothing compared to the bitter after-school arguments of the Speccy and Commie years!

Of course, the Spectrum never really took off anywhere other than the UK and small pockets of Europe. The Commodore 64 was a more international prospect, and still holds the world record for the most successful single unit home computer of all time, shifting as many as 17 million between 1983 and 1994, when it finally stopped production. Not bad for a chunky beige breadbin that cost a packet!

loading in peace

The Commodore 64 had another big advantage over the Spectrum – it used Commodore's own brand tape player, which meant there was no piercing data screech while waiting for your game to load!

INTERNATIONAL KARATE+

Three-way combat and slapstick jokes make for a true belter of a fighting game!

ONE of the most exciting things about those first few years of home gaming was that the popular genres had yet to fully take form. There were games about driving, games about fighting, games about shooting, but each one had very different ideas of how to realise those ideas for players.

That's what makes 1987 hit *International Karate+* still stand out today. It's a fighting game that is unlike any other fighting game since, because it manages to be both a fairly sensible recreation of martial arts as a sport, and also a truly weird slapstick comedy game full of bouncing balls and schoolboy humour.

Written by Archer MacLean, *IK+* features not two but three fighters, all in combat against each other at the same time. There are no health bars, just the need to score six points from the referee before time runs out. You do this not with ludicrous Hadouken fireballs, but with actual karate punches and kicks. It's surprisingly realistic.

MATCH OVER

That realism doesn't mean the game is dry though. In fact, *IK+* is perhaps the funniest fighting game ever. Not just for the chance to knock your friends on their bum, but for all the bizarre background details and quirky Easter eggs hidden in the game.

Which gags you got depended on which computer you had, but you might see Pac-Man wock-wock-wocking across the screen behind you, or a submarine periscope rising from the sea. Bonus rounds included using a shield – or possibly a dustbin lid – to fend off bouncing balls from both sides, or kicking bombs away before they exploded.

You could even type in swear words and the game would tell you off for being rude. Type one in a second time, and it would reset completely! The greatest feature, as any fan will tell you, was what happened if you pressed 'T' on the keyboard during a match. That made all the fighter's pants fall down, and was the perfect way to disrupt even the tensest multiplayer tournament. Mr. Miyagi definitely didn't teach that move. Pants on, pants off!

THE REST OF THE BEST

Not cool enough to own a Speccy or C64?
Well meet the alternatives…

Amstrad CPC 464

The Amstrad was the perpetual runner-up in the computer race behind Sinclair and Commodore's more popular platforms. It certainly wasn't a bad computer, but it lacked the eccentric brilliance of the Speccy and the confident oomph of the C64. It was just sort of… there. Pity the friend who got an Amstrad for Christmas, and ended up left out of the tape-swapping break time madness at school. Of course, Amstrad boss Alan Sugar had the last laugh – he ended up buying Sinclair from Sir Clive. You're fired!

BBC Micro

Even the BBC got into the computer market in the 80s, working with computer company Acorn to launch the ridiculously durable BBC Micro Model B. Every school had one of these – usually literally just one, in a corner of a spare room – and because they were designed to withstand daily school use, this was a computer that could probably survive a nuclear war (which was also a real possibility back then). Roughly the same size, weight and colour as a concrete paving slab, the BBC Micro's educational focus meant that most of its games were far too wholesome and sensible. How boring!

Dragon 32

Did you know anyone with a Dragon 32? Maybe you were that person with a Dragon 32? If so, cherish that fact, since it puts you in a very rare minority. The Dragon was a truly odd computer. It was actually one of the more powerful machines of its time, but it struggled to produce arcade graphics. To make matters worse, it's default display was green text on a dark green background. You might as well have tried programming a snooker table!

Acorn Electron

The BBC realised it needed a more affordable computer than the BBC Micro to compete with the ZX Spectrum, and so they produced the Acorn Electron, a cut-down version that could be sold cheaply. Trouble was, those cuts meant that the Electron looked and played like a Fisher Price toy, and couldn't compete in terms of speed, graphics or anything else. This was one acorn that didn't grow into a mighty oak: it was quietly dumped in 1985 after just two years on sale!

THE JOY OF TEXT

Infuriating puzzles, baffling phrases and purple prose –
welcome to the glorious world of text adventures…

WHAT do you do if you want to tell an epic story in a game, but the computers of the time simply can't handle the graphics needed? Simple. You make a text adventure, where all the action is written down, the player controls are verbs and nouns, and an occasional picture is all you need to set the scene.

LOOK. YOU SEE A LAMP. GET LAMP. I DON'T UNDERSTAND "GET LAMP". PICK UP LAMP. YOU PICK UP THE LAMP. LIGHT LAMP. I DON'T UNDERSTAND "LIGHT LAMP"…

This sort of riveting exchange was edge of the seat stuff for a certain gaming subculture, but while most game genres manage a revival or two as time goes by, the text adventure has remained dead and buried since the 1980s with apparently nobody crying out for it to return. That's understandable. Already lumbered with a reputation for appealing only to the beardiest, nerdiest fantasy aficionados at the time, for most players the slow pace and laborious spelling of the text adventure felt too much like homework.

That's not to say there weren't some good games to be found, but most used confusing inputs and indecipherable puzzles to mask the fact that, actually, the whole thing could be beaten in half an hour if you knew what to type in!

```
The nasty goblin captures you.
You are in the goblins dungeon
>< >< >< >< >< >< >< >< >< >< >< >< >< >< ><
> ENTER CRACK
 YOU CANNOT ENTER THE SMALL
INSIGNIFICANT CRACK.
> GO CRACK
+
```

The Rats

Yes, James Herbert's famous novel of rodent horror even got a text adventure! This one was split between a sort of strategy game, in which you had to coordinate London's response to the rising wave of killer rat attacks, and adventure sections based on chapters from the book where you had to help characters evade the gnawing critters.

The Hobbit

It's safe to say that the text adventure version of Tolkien's beloved fantasy epic cuts a few narrative corners. The Mirkwood forest is only a few screens away from Bilbo's front door, for one thing, but it manages to hit the edited highlights of the tale quite successfully.

The game is best remembered for the crude AI of its other characters, with Gandalf wandering in and out of scenes at random, and Thorin proving distractingly fond of sitting down and singing about gold every ten seconds!

The Incredible Hulk

There were three text adventures based on Marvel Comics superheroes. The Hulk's adventure starts with a puzzle that illustrates the frustrating nature of the genre. It opens with Bruce Banner tied to a chair, unable to do anything. The game won't start until you eventually work out that you must BITE LIP in order to make him turn into The Hulk...

NUGGETS...

So you think you know all there is to know about classic retro gaming? Try impressing your mates with these nuggets of info!

PONG

One of the earliest video games created, *Pong* was as simple as they came. Two players attempted to bat a pixel-shaped 'ball' back and forth, in a vain attempt to become the 'winner'. Yep, classic...

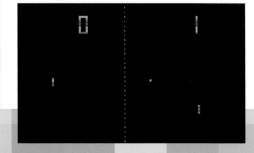

Q*BERT

Jumping into arcades in 1982, *Q*bert* was a 2D isometric game featuring a big-nosed orange blob on legs who appeared to swear a lot. This fan favourite character also appeared in the movie, *Wreck-It Ralph*.

JEFF MINTER

Legendary video game designer and programmer. Jeff created such iconic games as *Gridrunner*, *Hover Bovver* and *Tempest 3000*, as well the as the wacky *Attack of the Mutant Camels* and *Mama Lama*. Top bloke.

YIE AR KUNG-FU

The precursor to the likes of *Street Fighter*, this 2D arcade beat-em-up was published by Konami in 1985. Another of its fighters, *Martial Champion*, was planned to be released as *Yie Ar Kung-Fu*, but instead they created a brand-new game from scratch.

JR. PAC-MAN

When Pac-Mom and Dad are away, it's Jr.'s time to play! Er...yay? This obvious Pac-cash-in dropped on arcades in 1983 and featured such radical new gameplay improvements as double-width mazes and Jr's teeny-tiny red propeller hat.

KING & BALLOON

Namco's 1980 arcade shooter is prominent for one thing and one thing only: speech. In the Japanese version, the King says 'herupu' (Help!), 'sankyu' (Thank You!) and 'baibai' (Bye Bye!) in a very heavy Japanese accent.

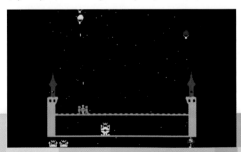

BURGER TIME

Created for its forgettable DECO Cassette System, Data East's tasty arcade game arrived in 1982. Players had to stack burgers, whilst dodging such food-based enemies as Mr. Hot Dog, Mr. Pickle and Mr. Egg.

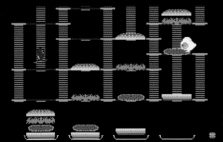

URIDIUM

Lose your lunch with the slipperiest shooter ever!

THE scrolling shoot-em-up was well established in arcades by the mid-80s, but home computers had struggled to match the eye-popping colours and relentless action made possible by a dedicated arcade machine.

Commodore classic *Uridium* did things a bit differently. Coded by Andrew Braybrook, instead of constantly scrolling horizontally or vertically across a level, each stage of the game was made up of one gigantic Dreadnaught spaceship. You, in your Manta fighter, had to speed across its surface, *Star Wars*-style, destroying its defences and dodging enemy attackers. Only when the enemy Dreadnaught was completely defenceless could you land on its hull and trigger the self-destruct sequence, before nipping off to tackle the next one.

With the ability to change direction, flitting left to right and back again, *Uridium* turned the shoot-em-up genre on its head. You could also collide with the 3D structures on the surface of each Dreadnaught, requiring fancy flying to squeak through gaps. It's this seat-of-your-pants nature that made Uridium stand out, and it still inspires fans even today. Modern indie hits *Futuridium EP* and *Hyper Sentinel* both make no secret of their debt to Braybrook's classic!

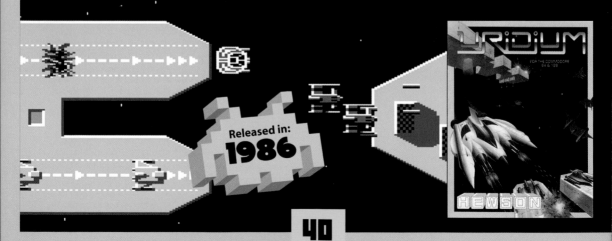

Released in:
1986

THE LAST NINJA

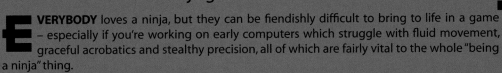

Released in: **1987**

Shuriken shenanigans in the best ninja game ever made!

EVERYBODY loves a ninja, but they can be fiendishly difficult to bring to life in a game – especially if you're working on early computers which struggle with fluid movement, graceful acrobatics and stealthy precision, all of which are fairly vital to the whole "being a ninja" thing.

The Last Ninja got it all right, offering an adventure that was more than just a relentless button-bashing action extravaganza, and instead let you feel like you really were creeping around in black jim-jams, trying to infiltrate the fortress of an ancient Japanese warlord.

Controlling agile ninja hero Armakuni, you get to somersault across raging rivers and clamber up sheer cliff faces, as well as using iconic ninjutsu gizmos like the bo staff, shuriken throwing stars and, of course, the nunchaku, a weapon so lethal it was banned from UK cinema screens in case we smashed our faces open with homemade broom handles and toilet chains.

Best of all, *The Last Ninja* let you target enemies in the legs, body or head. Admit it: you spent most of the game trying to whack the bad guys in the knackers...

· POWER ·

· WEAPONRY ·

THE LAST NINJA

CRASH, ZZAP, WALLOP!

Before the Internet, YouTube and Twitch, you had to go to shops for your gaming news…

IT'S no exaggeration to say that today's gamers are spoiled rotten. Not only can they buy, download and play the latest games without even putting on their pants, but they can watch hours and hours of full colour, high definition gameplay, streamed to the palm of their hand, before making a purchase. That's a far cry from the golden age of gaming magazines, when we'd have to wait a month for our next dose of gaming news and reviews, and had to decide whether to gamble our pocket money on a new game based on nothing more than magazine reviews accompanied by blurred black and white photos of the game running on an office telly.

Towards the end of the 8-bit computer era, most mags propped up their flagging circulation by giving away tapes full of free games. Eventually, you could get as many as seven full-price titles sellotaped to the front cover for nothing!

Launched in 1981, Computer and Video Games magazine stayed in print until 2004, and then lived on as a website until 2015, making it the world's longest surviving games media title!

And yet we loved them! While the early computer mags were as dry as barbecued Ryvita, the games magazines they spawned were as full of excitement and enthusiasm as the young gamers they were written for. In fact, in many cases, it was young gamers who were doing the writing! Piled in bedrooms, these dog-eared bibles would be obsessed over until the next issue, and then re-read whenever a fix of gaming news was needed.

The best (and worst) thing about old games mags was that they always had sections of games to type in to your computer yourself. Except you'd enter all the text, type RUN and it would immediately crash because of a misplaced semicolon somewhere in the listing. If nothing else, we learned how to cope with disappointment...

Stuck on a game? Tough! You'd have to wait and see if someone had found a cheat code, or written a POKE program to give you infinite lives. Or maybe you're lost? Rip some graph paper out of your maths book and draw a map yourself!

WAGGLE IT UNTIL IT BREAKS!

The greatness of joysticks… and the games that destroyed them!

EVER notice how nobody buys joysticks any more? Well, apart from dedicated fighting game competitors who demand an arcade-precise controller for the latest *Street Fighter*, or the devoted flight simulation player who wants to cement the illusion that they really are flying a 737 to Frankfurt. But once upon a time, everybody had a joystick. You could play on the keyboard, if you didn't mind revealing to the world that you were a lowly peasant, but anyone who took their gaming even a little bit seriously had to have a joystick of some kind.

And how many kinds there were to choose from! Kempston and Cheetah! Quickshot and Competition Pro! These were the technical terms that separated the hardcore from the casuals, long before hardcore and casual gaming was even a thing.

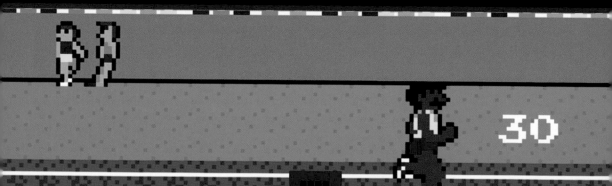

Cheetah Tortoise

Hardware manufacturers came up with all kinds of weird and wonderful controllers back in the day, but nothing could beat the Cheetah Tortoise for sheer strangeness. Shaped like an actual tortoise, you had to tilt his shell to control the on-screen movement. Needless to say, it did not catch on...

Some were short and stubby, perfect for fast, snappy movement. Others were long and lanky, allowing for finer control. As with everything game-related in the 1980s, debate raged as to which was best. In truth, of course, they all used the same binary microswitches, so any preference was down to personal taste rather than any subtlety in performance.

The only real joystick test that mattered was whether it could withstand a sweaty session of *Track & Field*, *Daley Thompson's Decathlon* or any of the other wrist-smashing sports games that were so popular back then. These were the games which took the peak of athletic endurance and training, and reduced it to how fast teenagers could waggle their joystick from side to side. The jokes wrote themselves. If you played those games, you'll probably have lost at least one joystick to enthusiastic exertions. There you are, seconds from the finish line in the 100m sprint when waggle, waggle, waggle... CRUNCH. Disaster. There's something rattling around inside the casing, and moving left has no effect. Game over. You may have lost that race, but at that moment you also joined an elite pantheon: the gamers who gamed so hard they their stick. Respect.

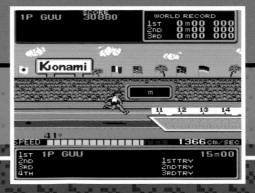

THE AWESOME 80s!

Films, TV shows, cartoons and comics…
these are the spin-off games that defined a decade!

OCEAN Software was famous for its TV and movie tie-ins, making games based on everything from *Knight Rider* to *Top Gun*. Both of the 80s biggest action stars appeared in Ocean games, with Stallone headlining *Rambo* and *Cobra*, while Arnie muscled his way into *Red Heat*.

Ocean's most infamous game was *Street Hawk*, which was so delayed that they had to quickly produce a cheap version to satisfy people who had pre-ordered the game as a gift for subscribing to Crash magazine. This version of the game is now so incredibly collectable, it regularly sells online for more than £50!

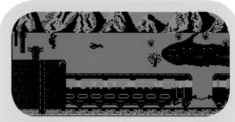

US Gold specialised in games based on hit US TV shows. *Airwolf, The Fall Guy* and *The Dukes of Hazzard* all got the game treatment, but were notoriously difficult. They also had very little in common with the shows. For example, *The Fall Guy* opens with a pot-bellied stick man jumping up and down on top of a train, dodging a vulture. Now, we're not sure Lee Majors ever did that!

e 80s was a golden age of bombastic rtoon shows, featuring heroes with ankly obscene muscle mass and super uman strength. A gaming dream. eryone loved *He-Man*, *Transformers* d *Thundercats*, but who remembers *avestarr*, *Centurions* and *M.A.S.K.*?

One of the most prolific TV-to-games stars was Danger Mouse. The daredevil super-spy rodent starred in three intriguingly named games: *Double Trouble*, *Making Whoopee* and *The Black Forest Chateau*.

Despite being one of the biggest TV hits of the 1980s, *The A-Team* struggled to cross over into gaming. The official game was a light gun shoot-em-up for the ZX Spectrum that was only released in Spain!

All the family could join in with games based on popular TV quiz shows. If the sight of a twitching pixelated Bob Monkhouse in *Bob's Full House* didn't scare the pants off you, there was always Paul Daniels in *Every Second Counts*, or Bob Holness in *Blockbusters*. Utterly terrifying.

Even little kids could get in on the action, with cheap and cheerful games based on *Postman Pat*, *SuperTed*, *Fireman Sam*, *Thomas the Tank Engine* and *Sooty* all available for a couple of pounds.

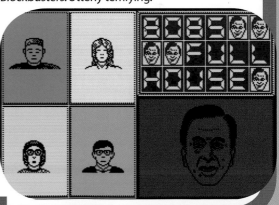

Released in:
1984

ELITE

Move over Han Solo, we've got a galaxy to explore!

THE BBC Micro may not have been the world's first choice for games, but it was still the computer that launched one of the most influential space simulators of all time. *Elite* cast you as a roving space pilot, and gave you a whole universe to explore. Whether you were battling the sinister Thargoids, ferrying goods between star systems or engaging in acts of galactic piracy, it was one of the first games to truly let the player decide what sort of hero they wanted to be.

OK, so the universe may have been made up of stark white shapes drawn on an inky black background, and your interactions with the other inhabitants little more than text boxes and laser blasts, but considering most games in 1984 were still working out how to make the screen scroll from left to right, *Elite* remains a phenomenal achievement and one that obsessed an entire generation of science fiction gamers.

zero to anti-hero

If you had an end goal in *Elite*, it was to go from being ranked Harmless at the start of the game, all the way up to the *Elite* rank of the title. Or you could just fly around, delivering textiles to aliens. Up to you.

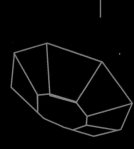

that's novel

Elite was the first game to have its own spin-off book, shipping with a novel called *The Dark Wheel* which followed a young pilot doing all the things players could also do in the game, while tracking down his father's killer.

dock, dock who's there?

Ask any veteran *Elite* player what the most important spaceship gadget was, and they'll all agree: the docking computer. Docking manually with a space station means lining up your ship with a rotating slot on the station. Get it wrong and you explode and die. Instantly. Pity the poor player who never mastered that particular manoeuvre!

elite lives on

Elite co-creator David Braben is still making games today and in 2014 released *Elite: Dangerous*, an updated multiplayer version of the game with state of the art graphics and virtual reality support. Braben also made the 2003 PlayStation 2 game *Dog's Life* in which, yes, you play as a dog and can not only poop at will, but sniff other dogs in the bum. Classy.

YO, HO, HO AND A LOT OF OLD ROM!

Couldn't afford computer games of your own?
Then a career in video piracy was right for you...

WHILE releasing games on cassette meant they could be produced quickly and cheaply in large numbers, there was also a downside: literally anyone with a tape-to-tape recorder could copy games just as fast, without the need for any software hacking at all.

This, of course, was the age of the ghetto blaster so there were few teenagers who didn't have a twin-deck beast of a machine ready to run off copies of their latest game for all of their mates. A games collection without at least a few dozen cheeky C-90 tapes full of hooky games was practically unheard of.

It was an imperfect crime though. Since tape games were temperamental loaders at the best of times, second generation copies – and even third, fourth and beyond – were even more precarious. Many an after-school evening was wasted trying to run off a working copy of *Ghosts n' Goblins* before teatime.

Of course, the games publishers quickly cottoned on and began dreaming up ways to make home-taped copies impossible to play.

Speed Loaders

One of the more effective methods of stopping piracy was the introduction of speed loaders. These were games that could shovel data into the computer's memory much faster, but also meant that mistakes in the tape-to-tape process were more pronounced.

Lenslok

This was a system used on the original release of space epic *Elite*, which involved using a special plastic lens to decipher an on-screen pass code needed to start the game. Trouble was, the lens was rubbish – and results varied depending on the size and shape of your TV screen. Loads of people bought Lenslok games legitimately, but still couldn't play them!

Look it up!

1984 text adventure *Mindwheel* was the first to use the instruction manual as a form of copy protection. Players would have to look up a random word on a random page of the accompanying book in order to access the game. Resourceful pirates didn't take long to figure out you could just photocopy every page – which took ages, but even pirates had patience back then. Yaaar!

AN ELECTRONIC NOVEL

MINDWHEEL

Colour coding

If pirates were going to photocopy material designed to stop them, then game publishers were going to come back with things that couldn't be photocopied, such as *Jet Set Willy*'s brightly-coloured code sheet. Useless in black and white, this fold out giant looked like modern art – and ensured that copying this particular classic was more trouble than it was worth!

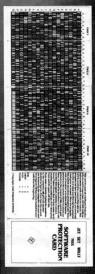

GAMES WITHOUT GLAMOUR

Who wouldn't want to play a game about being a binman?

WE take it for granted today, but there was a time when simply being able to move a little figure around on the TV seemed like some sort of advanced sorcery. The telly was where Wogan and Bergerac did their thing! Not where YOU could be in control!

That novelty factor meant that many early games simply looked to real life for their inspiration, safe in the knowledge that the experience would still be pretty amazing and magical for the player. How else to explain these titles, which turned mundane everyday jobs into interactive entertainment?

Paperboy

The humble paper round was a particularly unusual chore to turn into a game, especially since most of its target audience probably raised the money to buy the game by doing the job emulated in the game. Woah.

Tapper

Arcade classic *Tapper* may be more inspired by American bars than British pubs, but it still turned the serving of foaming pints and the collecting of empty glasses into a frantic panic-stricken race against time. Amazingly, they didn't bother with a bonus round where you had to unblock the gents because someone had sicked up a kebab.

Trashman

One of the most unapologetically unglamorous and unexciting games ever made, *Trashman* is exactly what it sounds like. You empty bins. And that's it. Trudging along behind the dustbin lorry, hurrying down garden paths to collect and return the bins, the peril is supplied by the fact that sometimes you get mauled by dogs or killed by a passing car. The bonus is that some residents give you a cash tip – which the game then scolds you for accepting.

Mrs Mopp

This depressing ZX Spectrum game casts you as a stressed out housewife, desperately trying to keep the kitchen clean while malevolent poltergeists materialise rubbish and dirty crockery all over the floor. Luckily, if the daily grind gets too much you can always perk Mrs Mopp up by drinking gin (yes, really) but should she become too worn out she has a nervous breakdown and leaves home. This is what passed for kid's entertainment in 1983.

Auf Wiedersehn Pet

Yes, even the classic comedy about Brit bricklayers in Germany got its own game, in which you build a wall, go to the pub and then stagger home avoiding the police. For maximum realism, the cover didn't even feature the cast of the show – just a photo of a couple of builders who can't even be bothered to face the camera!

THE SAD SAGA OF WALLY WEEK

Welcome to the bleakest gaming franchise ever conceived!

TAKE a look at the gaming characters who endure across multiple titles in a series, and you'll notice they generally have one thing in common: they're all cool, or fun, or fun and cool at the same time.

Meet the guy who breaks the trend: Wally, a hapless working class everyman who, along with his equally ordinary family, somehow starred in five games between 1984 and 1985. Wally didn't have super powers, and he didn't save kingdoms from monstrous enemies. He rescued precisely zero princesses and won no intergalactic wars. He just tried to get by. And we, the lucky playing public, got to help him.

In his first game, *Automania*, you had to help him build cars in the factory where he worked. Climbing and jumping around the levels, you collected the parts for a series of cars, from a humble Volkswagen Beetle to a fancy Rolls Royce. Wally, of course, didn't get to drive any of them.

In the follow-up, *Pyjamarama*, you must simply get Wally to wake up and get to work. You do this by navigating the freakish lucid nightmare that is his subconscious mind, in which his humble suburban home becomes a gauntlet of hazards and puzzles.

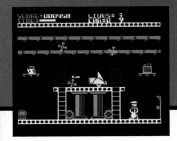

Everyone's a Wally came along next, and introduced Wally's family and friends. One of the first games to feature multiple playable characters, each had their own puzzles and tasks but the prize at the end was nothing more than the wages they'd already earned. In a particularly dispiriting twist, contact between Wally and his infant son Herbert saps his energy. Yes, being a parent literally brings Wally closer to death. Delightful. Herbert took centre stage for the next in the series – *Herbert's Dummy Run* – before the franchise came to an end with *Three Weeks in Paradise*, in which the cheap package holiday that they've slaved to earn becomes yet another trial of wits, as Wally has to rescue his wife, Wilma, and Herbert from some frankly racist cannibal stereotypes.

This was the fantasy being sold to gamers in the mid-80s: a life of soul crushing toil for meagre pay, in the hopes of earning a holiday that turns out to be the worst thing ever. The *Wally Week* games were basically a depressing Ken Loach social drama, played out with platform jumping and obscure inventory items. Have fun!

Everyone's a Wally

Everyone's a Wally even came with its own theme song, performed by actor and pop star Mike Berry and recorded on the B-side of the game cassette!

METROID

A sprawling sci-fi action epic with a twist in the tale…

IN *Metroid,* players first took on the role of Samus Aran, a cosmic bounty hunter fighting to prevent villainous space pirates from using alien parasites known as Metroids to rule the galaxy. The original game was set on the planet Zebes and ended with Samus battling the monstrous Mother Brain.

Metroid was notable for two distinct reasons, the most notable of which was that it was one of the first console games to offer a truly non-linear gameplay experience. Whereas other games featured levels which scrolled in one direction until you reached the end, the *Metroid* map spread in all directions and could be explored in any way the player wanted. Along the way, you could acquire new gadgets and abilities, which would allow you to enter areas that were previously off limits.

As a result, there were lots of potential paths through the game and multiple endings, making completion less of a one-off victory and more of a flexible journey that could be repeated in different ways.

Metroid's other memorable feature only became apparent once a good ending had been reached. In the final scene, the heroic Samus removes their helmet and spacesuit to reveal that – shock horror – she's a woman. Yes, the 1980s was an era when the idea of a playable female character was rare enough to be considered a major plot twist. And she still had to get her kit off to prove the point!

There have been 12 *Metroid* games in total, and Samus Aran has also turned up in the Super Smash Bros. fighting games!

Released in:
1986

EXCITEBIKE

Get your motor running in this wild motocross classic!

nOT every Nintendo franchise took place in whimsical or fantastical settings. 1984 classic *Excitebike* is based on the very real sport of motocross racing, and although it never quite lives up to its title is still one of the most enjoyable motorbike games even today!

It's a simple left to right race over ramps and other obstacles, with a few quirky twists to the formula. There were two accelerators, for example, the second of which gave you a much faster boost at the expense of a rapidly overheating engine. Let it get too hot and your bike conks out, allowing other racers to overtake.

You also had to be careful with your landings, angling the bike in mid-air to avoid losing speed when you hit the ground – or even flying over the handlebars.

Best of all, *Excitebike* let you design your own courses – although in the west that feature came with one serious drawback. The Japanese NES had an external tape recorder that allowed data to be saved. The US and UK didn't get this attachment, so while *Excitebike* teased players with options to save and load their creations, there was no way to actually do it! All you could do was switch off and lose all that hard work. Agony!

Released in:
1984

GAMES GO POP!

Even the lamest celebs had their own games in the 1980s!

IT'S not much of a surprise that movie action heroes and cartoon superstars turned up in games. After all, their adventures were perfect for such interactive escapades. Harder to explain are the multiple examples of pop stars starring in games, which often resulted in very strange experiences…

Frankie Goes To Hollywood

Holly Johnson's provocative pop group not only starred in their own game, it was really good! The game casts you as an average person who must become interesting enough to be given the mysterious Frankie's blessing, at which point you ascend to the Pleasuredome. A weird mix of suburban adventure game and surreal arty mini-games, it's almost certainly the only 8-bit game to feature both sperm and Nazi bombers.

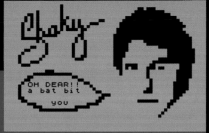

Shaky Game

Tucked away at the end of Side 2 of the 1983 Shakin' Stevens album 'The Bop Won't Stop' was *The Shaky Game*, a ZX Spectrum maze in which you had to guide Shaky's car past a pair of angry bats, for some reason, to the old house from his chart hit, 'This Ol' House'. "Oh dear a bat bit you" is the message that accompanies the pixel face of the Welsh rocker, which only appears when you die. How bizarre.

The Thompson Twins

This quirky pop trio starred in their own text adventure, which was given away free to in CVG magazine as a 7" flexidisc, which then had to be taped before you could load the game. When you did, you got a short game in which the lyrics of the song 'Doctor Doctor' inspire a quest to deliver potion ingredients to a witch doctor who lives up a mountain. Those who could figure out this task could win concert tickets. Lucky them.

Wham: The Music Box

It's not really a game but somebody somewhere decided that this powerful music creation software would sell better if it featured George Michael and Andrew Ridgely on the cover, and beepy renditions of hits like 'Club Tropicana' and 'Freedom' were already included to remix.

The Biz

A rare example of a star coding their own game, *The Biz* was written by Chris Sievey as a way of exorcising his own frustrations with pop stardom following the demise of his first band, The Freshies. A pop music management game, it oozes with depressed resentment at the petty hurdles that trip bands up, but the tape did feature the first recorded work by Sievey's more famous alter ego, Frank Sidebottom.

THEY MADE A GAME ABOUT WHAT?

Here's proof that you could make an 8-bit video game about literally any old rubbish!

Weetabix versus The Titchies

VERSUS THE TITCHIES

A unique computer game exclusively from Weetabix

Today the humble Weetabix is seen as a sensible breakfast, but back in the 80s for some reason they were advertised as a gang of skinheads led by Bob Hoskins. And what better way to support this strangely belligerent fibre-delivery system than with a cereal-themed mail order *Space Invaders* shooter in which a Weetabix defends the Earth from "The Titchies". Whatever they were...

Starring Charlie Chaplin

Games companies were so desperate for marketable names to base games on, that publisher US Gold even licensed the rights to a silent movie slapstick comedian from the 1920s. In the game, you control Chaplin in various different movie scenarios and ensure that each scene is sufficiently hilarious. The way you do this is by pushing everybody over onto their bums. Classic comic genius.

The Muncher

This snack-inspired game was based on the TV ads for Chewits. Just as the delightful animated dino munched on Barrow-in-Furness bus depot on the TV, so you controlled a giant green dinosaur smashing its way through a series of cities and army bases. The monster in the game looked nothing like the Chewits mascot because the game wasn't meant to be connected to a fruit sweet brand at all. Cheeky.

Sabrina

Busty Italian glamour model and popstar Sabrina even got a game of her own. This Spanish-only release was, bizarrely, a scrolling beat-em-up in which you guided the top-heavy starlet through a gauntlet of enemies ranging from prudish old women to leering men. Wearing only "small pants and a bare body" according to the instructions, Sabrina fends off her attackers in exactly the way you'd expect: she whacks them with her boobs....

The Comet Game

Halley's Comet only passes by the Earth every 70 years or so, but that tenuous link was enough to justify a computer game based on the celestial body when it swung our way in 1986. It's a baffling mish-mash of mini-games, none of which have anything to do with the actual Halley's Comet, and you mostly just had to make coffee for astronauts and shoot "space germs".

SHMUP, UP AND AWAY!

Ah, remember the golden years of arcade blasting, dodging, weaving, diving and 'shmuping'?

BACK in the late 80s, there was really only one way to prove you were a gaming genius and that was to excel at one of the ferociously difficult shoot-em-ups flooding the arcades from Japan. Whether they scrolled horizontally, or vertically up the screen, these were the games that really challenged you to make every credit count. Failure came fast, and only the best of the best got to add their initials to the high score table.

One of the reasons these games were so addictive was because while hard, they were never impossible. The best of the genre were exquisitely designed obstacle courses, made up of grotesque aliens and dozens of spiralling bullets, through which a talented player could nimbly pass, like a ballerina wielding a plasma cannon. That's because while home computers had limited processing power, meaning most home shooters simply threw random enemies at the player, arcade cabinets had dedicated circuit boards so each level, each wave of attacks, could be designed right down to the last pixel and repeated every game. With fast reactions, perseverance and a massive stack of 10p coins, it was possible (if not likely) for any player to get better and even beat the toughest shmups.

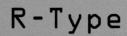

R-Type

In many ways Irem's *R-Type* was the granddaddy of the shmup genre. From its surreal screen-sized boss enemies to the wild array of power-ups and a beam weapon that could be charged to demolish everything in your path, this classic mixed amazing visuals with a relentless strategic challenge. It was one of the best shooters in the 80s, and it's still one of the best today.

Xevious

Zeevious? Ecks-ay-vee-us? However you pronounced it, this 1982 Namco classic was one of the earliest shmups and also one of the most innovative. Not only were you shooting at enemies flying towards you, but you were also bombing targets on the ground below. At a time when *Pac-Man* was still state-of-the-art, this multi-layered approach to action was nothing short of miraculous!

1942

Not every shooter was sci-fi themed. Williams scored a huge hit with this WW2 shooter that had you piloting a fighter plane over Pacific islands, gunning down bombers and other airborne menaces along the way. Best of all was the emergency dodge manoeuvre, in which your plane performed a deeply satisfying loop the loop. Admit it: you kept doing that even when you didn't need to, just because it looked cool.

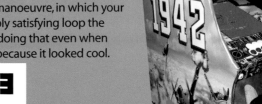

CASTLEVANIA

Konami's creepy classic gave the world a new way to play and a timeless quote…

IF you need a bad guy for your epic horror fantasy action adventure series, you might as well put all your own half-baked character ideas to one side and just go back to the source: Count Dracula. That's what Konami did in 1986 and the result was *Castlevania*, a series that inspired a whole new genre and featured at least one, now immortal, line of dialogue.

You played as Simon Belmont, last in a long line of vampire killers now hot on the trail of Dracula himself. Armed with nothing but a chain whip to defeat enemies and dislodge health and power ups from the scenery (they're particularly fond of hiding in candles, for some reason) it's up to you to save the world from the legendary bloodsucker's evil plan.

The first game in the series was a fairly straightforward platform game, in which Belmont plodded through fixed levels in order to do the deed. It was in the many *Castlevania* sequels and spin-offs that things started to get really interesting.

The first *Castlevania* sequel, which was developed at the same time as the original and was also the first to be released in Europe under the title *Vampire Killer*, blew open the linear platforming and instead offered a map you could explore at will. Imagine that!

The next follow-up, officially dubbed *Castlevania II: Simon's Quest*, went even further. Not only could you explore the castle in whatever order you wanted, using a completely open map, but you could get away form it all by having a day out at neighbouring towns, stocking up on some essentials while there. It even boasted a consistent day and night cycle, with different characters appearing in different places according to the time of day. *Castlevania III* took things further still, with a storyline that served up different gameplay sections depending on the choices you made.

Along with *Metroid*, *Castlevania* pioneered a world of player freedom. Almost a home from home, well, minus the vampires... That's why this style of side-scrolling open world exploration is still referred to today as "Metroidvania". Not a bad legacy!

While the *Castlevania* series got lots of things right, dialogue was never its strength. The 1997 PlayStation sequel, *Symphony of the Night*, features one of gaming's best loved cheesy lines which comes when hero Richter confronts Dracula with the news that mankind doesn't want his protection. "What is a man?" scoffs Dracula while gulping wine. "A miserable little pile of secrets!" Then they have a big fight. Classic drama!

Released in:
1986

THE REBIRTH OF NINTENDO

Back in the day, Nintendo launched its Famicom and strangely abbreviated console names were here to stay…

WHILE the UK was obsessed with 8-bit computers, and America was still reeling from the rapid rise and fall of Atari, a quiet revolution was taking place in Japan, courtesy of Nintendo.

Although most knew it for *Donkey Kong*, Nintendo had actually been around for a very long time. First founded way back in 1889 as a playing card company, Nintendo only started to look into electronics in the 1960s as it desperately looked for new business opportunities to keep it afloat. After distributing the Magnavox Odyssesy console in Japan, idealistic young engineers Gunpei Yokoi and Shigeru Miyamoto were tasked with investigating this exciting new market for "video games".

1983 saw the launch of Nintendo's first Family Computer, or Famicom, console. It took another two years for the device, now renamed the Nintendo Entertainment System or NES, to reach the USA, and it wasn't until 1986 that it started to show up in Britain and Europe.

In order to woo American gamers who had been burned by the collapse of Atari, Nintendo went out of its way to ensure that the NES looked nothing like the games consoles that had come before. Out went the mock-wooden panels, and in came a chunky futuristic white-and-grey design. Out went stubby joysticks and in came the first rectangular joypad controller. Truly a pad of joy.

Most especially, the NES was designed to function more like a VHS player, which at the time was the very height of home entertainment luxury. Cartridges no longer simply slotted into the top like a toy, but were instead gently slipped into a hatch on the front and then pressed down to connect the cartridge pins to the circuit boards inside the console. Fancy! This may have looked and felt much more satisfying and stylish than the old clunk-click Atari method, but those poor little pins didn't stand a chance against the eager 1980s gamer. Over time they would bend, making games harder to load. You would also find yourself having to routinely blow dirt and dust from the cartridge connectors to get some older games to work.

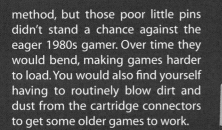

Other business ideas that Nintendo tried out during the 1960s and 1970s include a taxi company, a TV network, a range of instant rice snacks, and even a chain of "love hotels" where amorous couples could rent rooms by the hour. It's true!

The NES was ahead of its time in many ways. Although never released outside of Japan, it boasted such modern attachments as a modem for connecting to other services, and even an early virtual reality headset called the Famicom 3D System!

IT'S-A HIM, MARIO!

The journey of one anonymous jumping man from throwaway sprite to gaming icon…

WE all know who Mario is. Of course we do. He's just always been there, one of the few gaming heroes to have stayed the same over more than three decades; the cheery red cap, the bushy moustache, the upbeat can-do attitude. He's Mario!

But back in the beginning he was a humble carpenter known as Jumpman, the anonymous hero of *Donkey Kong* who leaped over barrels and scrambled up ladders to save his girlfriend from the rampaging ape. In fact, in the game's official storyline, Kong was Jumpman's pet who turned on his master after being "mistreated" – a dark twist that certainly puts their subsequent decades of rivalry in a sinister new light!

Mario was almost called 'Mr Video'!

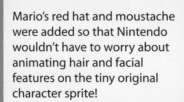

Mario's red hat and moustache were added so that Nintendo wouldn't have to worry about animating hair and facial features on the tiny original character sprite!

Mario is named after American businessman Mario Segale, who owned the warehouse space used by Nintendo when it was converting *Donkey Kong* for the US market. He impressed Nintendo employees by arguing with company president, Minoru Arakawa, about the rent!

What is Mario's full name? The title *Mario Bros.* implies that Mario is both his and Luigi's surname, making him Mario Mario. Nintendo has gone back and forth on confirming this, saying in 2012 that he had no official surname, but then in 2015 changing its story and admitting that, yes, he really is called Mario Mario. So now you know (until they change it again!)

Mario was finally given a name, a brother and a game of his own, in 1983's *Mario Bros.* which saw him teamed with Luigi for the first time. Now set in the sewers under New York, his occupation was changed from carpenter to plumber to explain why he was clanging around with underground pipes, and the rest is history!

Mario quickly became Nintendo's most prominent character, appearing in cameos in other games and headlining his own blockbusting series of platform games. He also starred in some unlikely, and largely forgotten spin-offs, including a range of educational titles and even *Super Mario Sweater*, an NES "game" that let you design your own knitted Mario which would then be made and delivered to your house!

NOW YOU'RE KNITTING WITH POWER.

SEGA MASTER SYSTEM

SEGA takes on Nintendo and a legendary rivalry begins!

THE Beatles or The Rolling Stones? Coke or Pepsi? *Eastenders* or *Coronation Street*? Pop culture has always had its epic taste-defining rivalries, and the battle between SEGA and Nintendo for the hearts of gamers around the world is one of the biggest.

The NES was already well established by the time SEGA launched its rival Master System, but it was SEGA's machine that offered the most gaming muscle for your money. It was faster, more colourful and more detailed – yet that wasn't enough to topple Nintendo from the throne. Why not? Because Nintendo had cunningly asked most game publishers to agree to contracts which prevented them from releasing their games on other machines, which meant that SEGA was stuck with a powerful console, but very few big name games to play on it. Ouch!

It didn't help that the early Master System model was a confused beast, with games available on both chunky cartridges and slim "SEGA Cards". These little cards could be sold at a lower price, but also couldn't contain more than 256k of code compared to 4Mb on a cartridge, and were quickly abandoned once it became clear that gamers wanted bigger and better games, not smaller and cheaper. While the Master System struggled to make its mark in Japan and the US, it eventually beat the NES in the UK and Europe, where most gamers were comparing it to Spectrum and Commodore rather than Nintendo's console. The Master System went on to sell 13m consoles worldwide, but the NES sold over 60m. Nintendo had won this time, but this was only their first battle…

Kidding Around

Pop quiz: who is SEGA's mascot? If you're thinking of a certain speedy blue hedgehog then it's a honking buzzer for you. The answer is actually Alex Kidd. This freakish gnome-like character, who looks like a cross between Liam Gallagher and Chucky, starred in six games between 1986 and 1990. Most of them were distinctly *Mario*-esque platformers, except for a Japan-only *BMX Trials* spin-off in which Alex rode the achingly popular 1980s stunt bike.

Although he never starred in another game following the ninja crossover title *Alex Kidd in Shinobi World*, SEGA still has fond feelings for the little guy. He's a playable character in *SEGA Superstars Tennis* and the *Sonic & SEGA All-Stars Racing* games, and has made cameo appearances in everything from kitsch dancing game *Space Channel 5* to action adventure *Shenmue*. Maybe a comeback isn't so unlikely after all…

A fantastically patronising bright pink "Master System Girl" was released in Brazil to entice more female gamers. It's doubtful that Sony or Microsoft would get away with that today!

OUT RUN

Get yer motor running, get out on the highway…

WE were easily pleased in 1986. Our dreams were simple. A bright red Ferrari Testarossa convertible and a clear blue sky? That was the life to aspire to. If you had those, everything would be amazing, forever.

SEGA gave us the chance to have those things for the price of a few coins shovelled into a slot. *Out Run* was not only the first driving game to ditch the idea of real world racing in favour of blasting around sunny Californian-esque tracks against the clock, but it let you sit in a real Ferrari to do it.

OK, not quite. You sat in a miniature car, the sort of thing a toddler might pester to sit in at the entrance to a supermarket. Except *Out Run* didn't slowly gyrate to the theme from *Postman Pat*, it gave you a steering wheel, a gear stick and pedals – and a glowing screen which transformed your frankly demeaning situation into a liberating blast down a shimmering West Coast highway.

In terms of actual driving mechanics, *Out Run* was just OK. In terms of racing, it had no competitors and only a time limit to beat. What it really did well was indulge the imagination, pandering to an 80s mindset drunk on advertising and pop videos, making you the cool dude with the best car.

Released in:
1986

Drive Time

Out Run was not only the first arcade game to let players choose the soundtrack, it was one of the first games where the soundtrack was something you'd want to listen to. SEGA's in-house composer Hiroshi Kawaguchi came up with four classic tracks – 'Passing Breeze', 'Splash Wave', 'Magical Sound Shower' and 'Last Wave' – and they're still as cool today as they were in 1986. So cool, in fact, that a vinyl album of tracks from the series was released in 2016!

Feeling the burn

Out Run pioneered the era of "sit down" games, as companies fought to keep gamers in the arcade with eye-catching cabinets, rather than playing on consoles at home. SEGA produced lots of similar titles: *Hang-On* let you sit astride a motorbike, while *Thunderblade* gave you a helicopter pilot seat. Best of all was jet fighter game *After Burner*, which came in an enclosed cockpit which rotated and tilted as you played. Pass the sick bag!

PLAYING WITH POWER!

Nintendo gives players a hand – literally!

LOCKED into its rivalry with SEGA, and still trying to reassure gamers who had been burned by Atari's collapse, Nintendo came up with some pretty hare-brained ideas to keep people interested in the NES. The Nintendo Power Glove is the perfect example, a pointless control method designed only to look cool but which actually made playing games even harder and more frustrating. As the name suggests, it was literally a big rubbery glove with a modified NES controller stuck on the wrist.

Additional features allowed the user to program different functions for different buttons, but the real selling point was the ability to control games just by moving your hand. It didn't really work, of course. By the time the Power Glove reached the shops it had been stripped down to such a degree that it could only register the most basic of finger movements – and even then, it wasn't very reliable.

The Power Glove has a memorable cameo in the 1989 movie *The Wizard*, produced by Nintendo. In the film, three kids go on an adventure across America to compete in a gaming tournament. Along the way they meet arrogant pro-gamer Lucas Barton who uses a certain controller. "I love the Power Glove," he gushes. "It's so bad!" While he was using the late eighties street slang where bad meant good, it was actually just rubbish.

MEET R.O.B!

Hi-tech gloves were nothing compared to your own robot gaming partner!

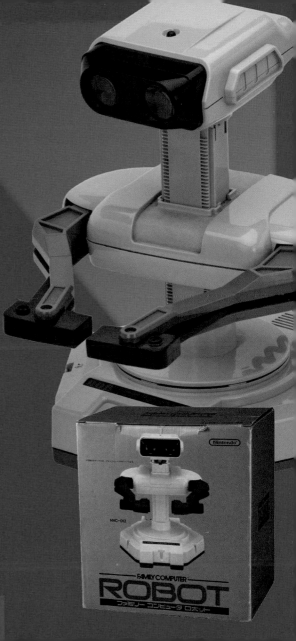

F the Power Glove seemed cool to 1980s kids, just think how awesome R.O.B. must have looked. Yes, this was Nintendo's Robotic Operating Buddy, who would sit by your side and help you play games. Amazing, right? Well, the reality was inevitably disappointing. Much like the Power Glove, R.O.B. was severely limited in what he could do, and was only compatible with a few rubbish games. Rather than a cool sidekick, he was basically just a fancy way of pressing buttons on a second controller. Again, there were only two games that made use of R.O.B.. The first, *Gyromite*, was included when you bought R.O.B., and featured him raising and lowering gates in the game to let an absent-minded sleepwalking professor pass safely. *Stack Up* was a basic puzzle game in which the player sent messages to make R.O.B. stack plastic rings in real life. Neither was exciting or interesting, and so wide-eyed kids who thought they were getting their very own R2-D2 pal ended up with crushing disappointment. Consider it a life lesson.

THE WORST CONTROLLERS EVER!

Just when you thought gaming peripherals couldn't get any worse...

SEGA Activator

This baffling motion controller for the SEGA Megadrive used a plastic ring to send beams of light upwards. By standing in the middle and blocking those beams with your flailing arms and legs, you were supposed to be able to instantly become a master of fighting games such as *Mortal Kombat* and *Street Fighter*. No. You just looked like a twit.

Konami Laser Scope

Light gun games were a perennial favourite, but what if instead of a gun you used your actual face? That was the stupid question posed by this bit of kit, and the answer that came back was as daft as you'd expect. Wearing this "Voice Command Optical Targetting Headset" you could shoot enemies just by looking at them, and shout out commands that the game would follow. In reality, you just looked like you'd been attacked by a Fisher Price hairdryer.

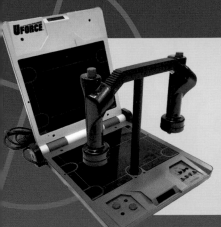

U-Force

For whatever reason, hardware companies seemed convinced that players really wanted to control their games without even touching a controller. That was the main selling point of the U-Force, which looked like a sandwich toaster but claimed to use infra-red beams to create a space where you could wave your hands about to control games. "Nothing comes between you and the game" growled the slogan. Given that quite often literally nothing would happen when you used it, that seems weirdly accurate.

Namco NeGcon

Don't think that ridiculous controllers were restricted to the distant past of gaming. This oddity was released for the original PlayStation in 1995, apparently on the basis that some players would rather twist their joypad in half than simply use a joystick or button. Supposedly created with driving games in mind, nobody at Namco thought it necessary to point out that steering wheels generally turn left and right, not backwards and forwards.

Coconuts Pachinko Controller

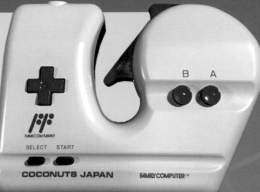

Check out this bizarre contraption. It might look like a device for extracting nails from a horse's hoof, but it was actually created solely for playing pachinko games on the NES. That trigger in the middle is spring-loaded and used to twang balls into play. Totally worth buying an entirely new joypad for!

LOST IN TRANSLATION

Could you repeat that, please?

As dozens of Japanese games were hurriedly converted to be played in the west, lots of effort was poured into ensuring the gameplay was recreated perfectly. It's just a pity that the same attention to detail wasn't always used on the dialogue and text…

Art of Fighting 2 (NeoGeo)

Fighting games have never been a particularly rich source of prose, with most of their storylines dished out in brief scenes and bizarre post-match slogans. That doesn't leave a lot of room for character development, but even the most forgiving player must stop and wonder what *Art of Fighting*'s King means when she celebrates the end of a match by declaring: "I am woman. Hear my kick and moan!"

Ghostbusters (NES)

If there's something strange in your neighbourhood, who you gonna call? Apparently not a proofreader, as completing the NES game based on the hit movie brings up the following garbled message: "Conglaturation !!! You have compelted a great game. And prooved the justice of our culture. Now go and rest our heroes!" Not even Bill Murray could make that line work.

Pro Wrestling (NES)

Sometimes the best examples of botched translation are the simplest. Take this classic early wrestling game, which famously celebrates every victory with the uplifting phrase "A Winner is You". Aw, thanks. And isn't we all, in some way, a winner? Yes we is.

Stop the Express (Sharp X1)

It's fair to say that without its legendary grammar-mangling celebratory message, this obscure train-based espionage action game would have long since been forgotten. Most people have never even heard of the computer it was first released on! And yet, thanks to the Internet, *Stop the Express* will always be remembered for telling us "Congraturation! You Sucsess!"

Zero Wing (Megadrive)

No discussion of weird translations would be complete without a tip of the cap in the direction of this home conversion of the Japanese arcade shooter. Yes, this is the game that gave us the timeless quote "All your base are belong to us."

X-Men (Arcade)

Not all of gaming's clunkiest lines are written down. Some are even spoken aloud. Take Konami's four-player *X-Men* arcade beat-em-up, in which supervillain Magneto taunts the heroic mutants by shouting "Welcome to die!" at them. And still nobody noticed that it didn't make sense.

LEMMINGS

Rescue tiny critters from grisly death in this puzzle classic!

ONE of the weirder short-lived fads of the early 16-bit era was a brief but memorable wave of incredibly popular games about little pixel creatures dying in horrible ways. And in this small ghoulish sub-genre, *Lemmings* rules the roost.

The aim of the game is simple. Hordes of mindless lemmings – or green-haired little things in blue leotards – drop into the level and must be guided to the exit without too many of them succumbing to the numerous fatal drops and traps that line their route. You have a limited number of powers to bestow on the lemmings, such as giving one the ability to block the others, to build a bridge or to explode, and must carefully plan the use of these resources to save the required number of innocent idiots.

With their squeaky voices and iconic minimalist design, each only a few pixels high, the lemmings were one of the breakout stars of the transitional Amiga years. Of course, the game spawned sequels – including unlikely spin-offs such as *Lemmings Paintball* and a platform game called *The Adventures of Lomax* in 1996 – but the series dropped out of favour in the early 2000s and has yet to make a comeback.

Maybe they all topped themselves after all?

Released in: 1991

WORMS

The humble garden minibeast goes Rambo!

WHILE players were tasked with saving *Lemmings,* a few years later more little pixel beasts were being blown to smithereens – and this time it was on purpose.

This best-selling series of multiplayer strategy games was created by amateur coder Andy Davidson, as an entry for a programming contest in Amiga Format magazine. It didn't win, but Yorkshire games developer Team 17 saw it and snapped it up, turning it into one of the longest running British gaming series of all time.

Each game features a team of heavily-armed worms taking it in turns to attack each other on 2D maps that were gradually eaten away by the mayhem. The series was famous for its bizarre weapons – such as the banana bomb and exploding sheep – as well as its oddball sense of humour. Each worm team had its own theme and high-pitched voices that yelped "Ooh, ya bugger!" after taking damage.

No less than 23 *Worms* games have been released, plus a *Worms* pinball game and a *Worms* golf game. Unlike *Lemmings*, this series has kept on ticking, with new entries released as recently as 2016. Turns out that worms really are more resilient than suicidal rodents after all…

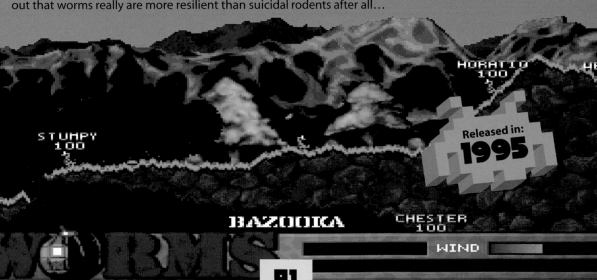

Released in: **1995**

ROLL UP!
ROLL UP!

How dragons, six-sided die and nerds changed the world –
and video games – forever…

YOU can't really talk about the origins of video gaming without acknowledging the parallel development of table top role playing games, or RPGs. Not only did many early video games draw inspiration from D&D, but it also spawned dozens of official video game adaptations and unofficially inspired hundreds more.

Created in 1974 by Gary Gygax and Dave Arneson, *Dungeons & Dragons* was a game played by friends, usually around a table, with each person creating their own character to undertake an adventure. That adventure was dictated by the Dungeon Master, who controlled the overall story and responded to player decisions based on a rapidly increasing set of official D&D rules. Basically a mixture of a Sunday league referee and your Dad reading you a bedtime story. The first official D&D interactive game was actually a hand-held electronic toy from Mattel released in 1981, but more detailed games quickly appeared for the Intellivision console, NES, SEGA Master System and every home computer you could think of. All told, there have been over 80 official *Dungeons & Dragons* video games over the years, and with more being made all the time, that rule book is bulging!

DUNGEONS & DRAGONS™
COMPUTER
FANTASY GA
MATTEL ELECTRONICS®

& DRAGONS

ic Medieval Wargames
e with Paper and Pencil
niature Figures

AX & ARNESON

3-VOLUME SET

Let this be your fantasy

Among the games to take inspiration from *Dungeons & Dragons* was a little Japanese game called *Final Fantasy*, first released in 1987. It featured a team of four friends exploring a hostile world full of monsters and magic and it demonstrated how the dice-rolling, nail-biting, seat-edging decisions and combat of tabletop role playing could translate to a screen.

Packaged with a breezy 84-page rule book, plus fold-out maps and monster guides, *Final Fantasy* was very much a traditional RPG. Hard to imagine when you compare it to the often bizarre and constantly changing mixture of science fiction, high fantasy and overblown Animé melodrama that the series is now known for!

Could it be (black) Magic?

Role playing games were so absorbing that they sparked a panic, particularly among American parents, who were afraid their kids would be lured into genuine black magic rituals by playing them. Stoking the parental panic fire, there was even a hilariously cheesy 1982 movie about the dangers of RPGs called *Mazes and Monsters*, starring a baby-faced new actor by the name of Tom Hanks!

OH MY GOD!

And on the seventh day, God created this lot...

AS games machines became more powerful, not every game designer wanted to use that extra muscle to make cars brum faster or guns more shooty. Some wanted to explore the big questions, to ponder life and death and how cool it would be to raise a volcano out of the ground with the click of a mouse. Peter Molyneux was one such designer, and in 1989 he released *Populous*, widely regarded as the first "God game".

As the name suggests, you play the role of an actual god, looking down on a little digital world populated by little people who mill about and exhibit basic artificial intelligence. You have the power to raise and lower the land, and from this basic interaction start to build up a suite of *Old Testament* powers with which to lead your tribe against their enemies. In the mood for a bit of smiting? Go nuts. Lob lightning bolts. Drop meteors. Cover everything in lava. It's all in a day's work for a deity.

Populous was an instant hit; quirky and fun, with a challenge not seen before in gaming. Needless to say, plenty of other games quickly sprang up to offer different approaches to the same idea…

Sim City

Published in the same year as *Populous*, Will Wright's *Sim City* wasn't quite a God game, more of a mayor simulator, but both games shared an omnipotent top-down view of the world, the ability to alter the lives of hundreds of pixel people and an obsession with natural disasters.

Sim Earth

The follow-up to *Sim City* was definitely taking a more Godly view of things. Now in control of the entire planet's ecosystem, it's up to you to nurture the development of intelligent life – or just destroy everything in an all-consuming hellfire.

Civilization

Pitched somewhere between the epic scope of *Populous* and the city management of *Sim City*, Sid Meier's 1991 strategy classic wanted players to think about more than just war and disaster. Playing as an historical leader, it's up to you to guide your empire from prehistoric basics through to conquering space, by developing language, science, religion and other social features.

Mega-lo-Mania

One of the more obvious *Populous* copycats, *Mega-lo-Mania* gave you more direct control over your subjects and placed more emphasis on the nuts and bolts of their development. Researching and building new weapons and technologies, you were less of an abstract celestial force and more of a warmonger's inspiration.

SWEET 16-BIT

The last gasp of the classic home computer era.

FOR most of the 1980s, gamers made do with 8-bits. Most didn't know or care what a bit was, or why computers and consoles only had eight of them, for that was how things were and nobody knew any different. But by the late 80s, word got around that there were some computers that had 16 bits. Double the power to do…whatever it was that bits do! Basically, these new computers were twice as good, twice as powerful and twice as fast as our dear friends, the Spectrum and Commodore 64. This was the future.

Technically these machines had been around since 1985, but were mostly seen as business machines. In 1987 Commodore released the 500 model of the Amiga, while Atari followed in 1989 with the enhanced version of its Atari ST computer. Both boasted superior graphical abilities, a previously unimagined dedicated joystick port and a growing library of games that were faster, slicker and bursting with more colour than a Rubiks cube.

The kids who had gleefully unwrapped a Spectrum or C64 on Christmas morning years before were now heading into their teens, and with Saturday job income augmented by pocket money, there was a generation primed to take the next big step towards a

proper grown-up computer as we'd know it today. Most noticeably, the Amiga and ST represented the first mass market computers – in Britain at least – to be controlled by a mouse. This was a feature common to business machines and early Apple computers, but for gamers it blew the gaming possibilities wide open.

Over the next few years gaming saw a decline in genres such as text adventures, replaced by graphics-driven adventure games where pointing and clicking on the scenery drove the story forward and moved the characters around. Simulation games were able to move to solid 3D graphics, while mouse control also meant that strategy games could start to shift away from ponderous turn-based grids and into real-time maps that could be spun and tilted and viewed from all angles.

It represented arguably the biggest leap forward in games technology ever seen, and in terms of sheer impact it has yet to be repeated. This wasn't just an incremental increase in the number of polygons or an invisible boost to frame rates. This was gaming's equivalent of the move from silent black and white movies to stereo technicolour widescreen, and almost every game genre you love today put down its roots in the 16-bit era.

THE SECRET OF MONKEY ISLAND

Grog, insults and a rubber chicken – it's the greatest adventure game ever made!

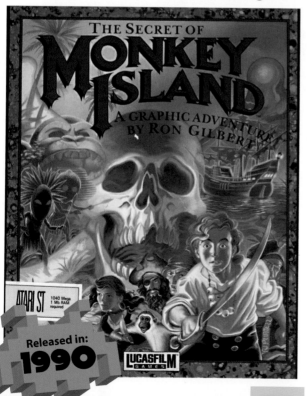

THE SECRET OF
MONKEY ISLAND
A GRAPHIC ADVENTURE
BY RON GILBERT

ATARI ST 1040 Mega
1 Mb RAM
required

Released in:
1990

LUCASFILM
GAMES

AS point and click mouse interfaces revolutionised gaming, the adventure genre felt that change more than most. No longer did players have to laboriously type in everything they wanted to do. Now they could click on an object and use it straight away. Added to this was the increasing graphical power of home computers, which meant that the occasional static illustrations of the early 1980s were now replaced with animated scenes, with characters that could walk around and do stuff.

One of the first companies to take advantage of this was Lucasfilm, first with *Maniac Mansion* in 1987 but most memorably with *The Secret of Monkey Island*, a laugh-out-loud pirate romp which not only cemented this new style of "graphic adventure" play but also proved that games could be as funny as a comedy movie.

Jack attack?

If the plot of *Monkey Island* sounds familiar, that's because it's also the same basic story as the first *Pirates of the Caribbean* movie. But since the first *Monkey Island* game was inspired by Disney's *Pirates of the Caribbean* theme park ride, that seems fair. Right?

You play as Guybrush Threepwood, a young man who yearns for pirate adventure. But in order to shiver his timbers, he must undertake a series of trials to prove himself, during which time he falls in love with Elaine Marley, the feisty governor of Melee Island, and does battle with LeChuck, a ghostly pirate.

There are many memorable features to the game, with the unusual combat system proving to be particularly fun. Rather than try to create an arcade-style sword fighting mini game, the programmers instead opted to have fights based around insults. Only by choosing the best insults and responses can you overcome your opponent. The game also features surreal and abstract puzzles, including one involving an infamous rubber chicken with a pulley in the middle – one of the weirdest in-game objects ever invented.

Monkey Island went on to inspire four sequels and was considered so influential it was chosen to appear in the Smithsonian American Art Museum!

By George!

Monkey Island was developed and published by Lucasfilm. Yes, the same company that made *Star Wars*. In fact, George Lucas himself has a cameo in the game. When you unmask the bridge troll, take a look at his beardy face and see if it looks familiar…

...NUGGETS...

SHAQ FU

When international basketball star Shaquille O'Neal wanted to appear in a video game, guess what kind of game it was? Yep, a beat-em-up, of course. Poorly conceived and released, this made *Space Jam* look like a work of art.

RISE OF THE ROBOTS

Infamous for being released on literally every single console platform available at the time, *Rise of the Robots* crashed and burned spectacularly. Released to cash in on the 2D fighting game heat of the time, this poor man's *Mortal Kombat* was scrap.

SOUTH PARK

Once reviewed as the 'worst game you've ever played', Comedy Central's *South Park* for N64 and PC should have been a big hit. Developed in collaboration with the show's creators, the game was a big Mr Hankey.

CARMAGEDDON 64

Developed by Titus for the N64 and based on the popular PC franchise of the same name, *Carmageddon* suffered from poor controls and terrible graphics. It also holds the World Record for lowest-rated N64 game of all time.

HOTEL MARIO

Remember that time in 1994 when Nintendo released that *Mario* game on the Philips CD-i? Nope. Us neither. This terrible title arrived on the console after the big N's falling out with Sony over their proposed joint video game machine. Lucky Sony...

FINAL FANTASY XIV

A bit of an anomaly in Square Enix's usually mega-successful RPG series, *FFXIV* was a single player MMORPG. The game was so poorly received, Square Enix's then-CEO Yoichi Wada had to issue an apology for its terrible quality.

POSTAL III

The third in the series of excessively violent games was released by developer Running With Scissors in 2011. Sub-contracted out to a much smaller games company, the result was a buggy mess, that was almost immediately disowned by RWS.

TURN TO PAGE 92

Time was when books were the new video games...

TABLE top role playing games were all very well, but they had some obvious drawbacks. For one thing, they could go on for ages. For another, they did rather assume that you had a bunch of like-minded mates who were prepared to sit in the kitchen and pretend to be wizards.

For the more solitary fantasy connoisseur there was always the alternative "game books". The most famous of these were the iconic *Choose Your Own Adventure* books; a series which included a staggering 184 titles released between 1979 and 1998.

The idea was simple. Rather than reading a story through from beginning to end, readers were given the chance to make decisions at the end of chapters, flipping to different pages to continue their adventure until they reached the end – or died, which was often more likely.

This concept was combined with dice-rolling RPG mechanics in the *Fighting Fantasy* series, created in the UK in 1982 by Steve Jackson and Ian Livingstone. Now readers had a character sheet at the beginning of the book, which had to be filled in with pencil and updated as you went along. Of course, canny readers quickly worked out the ultimate cheat mode: turning back to the previous page and pretending that fatal choices hadn't been made after all! But where's the fun in that?

Going off book

Of course, just as D&D spawned computer game versions, so too did adventure game books. The *Fighting Fantasy* series was very prolific, with *Warlock of Firetop Mountain*, *Forest of Doom*, *Seas of Blood*, *Rebel Planet* and others getting interactive adaptations that combined text adventure with role playing combat. Some were even packaged with copies of the original book! Bonus!

Lone Wolf

As with any popular fad, there were plenty of game book series that were huge in the 80s but have since been forgotten. *Lone Wolf* added a darker pagan twist to the concept, while the *Way of the Tiger* books cast you as an avenging ninja. Both, naturally, also got computer game spin-offs!

Livingstone I presume?

Ian Livingstone not only co-created the *Fighting Fantasy* series, he was also instrumental in bringing *Dungeons & Dragons* to Britain and went on to be the boss of games publisher Eidos, bringing us such hits as *Tomb Raider*. Bravo, Ian!

POINT AND CLICK

Who needs fancy controllers when you have a mouse and a finger, right?

no celebration of the classic point and click adventures would be complete without acknowledging that some of them featured puzzles that were downright ridiculous. *King's Quest V* was particularly guilty of this sort of thing. At one point in the game, you're trapped in a time loop by a witch, forced to repeat the same screens over and over. How do you get out? You smear peanut butter on a specific spot on the floor and stick jewels in the peanut butter to attract a fairy to help you. Obviously.

At least that puzzle didn't kill you, unlike the moment in the game when a Yeti attacks and you have a few seconds to select an item from your inventory to save your life. Is it a sword? Or a shield? No. It's an apple pie. Really.

But at least you know you've failed that puzzle. In what is probably the worst puzzle ever in a game, there's a moment near the start of the game where you see a cat catch a mouse. A cute little background detail, you may think. But no. If you don't throw a shoe at the cat to save the mouse, you can't get a piece of rope that you need to get past a waterfall hours later. Yes, you can end up completely stuck, forever, for no reason. It's a miracle adventure games survived at all.

Beneath a Steel Sky

This 1994 classic had an ominous cyberpunk science fiction setting, a serious detective-driven storyline and featured a bonus comic book from *Watchmen* artist Dave Gibbons.

Space Quest

First released in 1986, this series of *Star Wars* spoofs featured six games, all starring Roger Wilco, a hapless janitor who accidentally gets caught up in intergalactic adventures.

Sam and Max Hit the Road

1993 brought this goofy hit, about a hyperactive rabbit and a private detective dog on the trail of a Bigfoot stolen from a carnival.

Broken Sword

This series of swashbuckling European adventures kicked off in 1996, and introduced players to George Stobbart, an American tourist, and Nicole Collard, a French journalist, both embroiled in a conspiracy involving the Knights Templar.

SONIC THE HEDGEHOG

What's blue, spiky and runs like the clappers?

ONE of the main reasons that the SEGA Megadrive was able to perform better against the SNES was that it finally had an exclusive game that people desperately wanted to play. Sorry Alex Kidd, off you trot. Here comes Sonic!

Right from the start Sonic was designed to be noticeably different to Mario. Rather than the cheery fairy tale whimsy of Nintendo's flagship games, Sonic was cool. Rather than copying Mario's steady waddle-and-jump gameplay, Sonic was all about speed. Rather than bopping enemies on the head with his bum, Sonic span into a ball of blue fury and smashed right through them. Hey, it was the early 90s. A rad attitude was exactly what gamers were looking for.

Created by programmer Yuji Naka, Sonic went through many design iterations before SEGA was convinced it had a character that could topple the Italian plumber. Early ideas included an armadillo, a rabbit that could grab things with its extra-long ears, and – somewhat randomly – a character based on former US president Theodore Roosevelt wearing pyjamas. While SEGA eventually settled on a super-fast blue hedgehog, many of these designs ended up finding their way into other games. And that weird pyjama president character? He became Sonic's arch enemy, Dr Robotnik!

In Japan, Dr Robotnik was known as Eggman, because of his plus-sized waistline. Hey Japan! Haven't you heard? Body-shaming isn't cool!

As well as being a video game icon, Sonic is a big comic book star. In the UK *Sonic the Comic* lasted for a whopping 223 issues, while his US comic earned a Guinness World Record by running for 290 issues over ten years!

The first *Sonic the Hedgehog* game created a template that has endured for over 25 years. Fast-paced platforming action, with intricately designed levels packed with secrets and short cuts. By revving Sonic on the spot, players can build up additional speed and race up ramps, loops and corkscrew tracks.

Along the way, Sonic, like all hedgehogs, collects golden rings which act as a sort of health bar. If he takes a hit, he carelessly drops the rings he's carrying. Every time. If he gets hit without any rings, he loses a life. Collecting 100 rings, of course, earns him an extra life. Phew.

That first game was easily the most popular on the Megadrive, shifting 15 million copies, while *Sonic* games in general have sold over 80 million worldwide. He was one of the first characters inducted into the Video Game Hall of Fame in 2005, and is still an instantly recognisable icon around the world. Nice work, blue!

Released in:
1991

Ding, ding! Round 2... FIGHT! SNES Vs

nINTENDO won the first round of its battle with SEGA pretty conclusively, with the NES outselling the Master System by tens of millions, but the rivalry really kicked up a notch as the 1990s rolled around.

For one thing, SEGA was determined not to get left behind again and beat Nintendo to the 16-bit console market by almost two years. The SEGA Megadrive debuted in Japan in 1988, made its way to the USA under the name SEGA Genesis, and hit the UK in 1990. That meant by the time Nintendo got its Super Famicom console out in Japan in 1990, SEGA's rival was already available around the world. It took another two years before Brit gamers could get their hands on the Super Nintendo Entertainment System, or SNES.

This was the first time console gaming really hit the UK in massive numbers. The NES and Master System had been available in Britain, but with the nation's gamers weaned on actual computers like the Spectrum and Commodore, the idea of a little plastic box that played games looked a bit toy-like.

That changed with the arrival of the SNES and Megadrive, each of which was capable of finally replicating arcade style graphics whilst allowing gameplay in your slippers and pants, if so desired. A further bonus, of course, was that cartridge games loaded as soon as you switched them on. No more tapes and discs!

MEGADRIVE

When SEGA launched it's previous console (the Master System), Nintendo insisted on publishers launching games exlusively for its machine, but that wasn't the case this time. This meant that the biggest arcade conversions and movie tie-ins were available on both the Megadrive and the SNES. The competition was REAL.

Instead, the companies used hardware to try and win over gamers and keep console sales high. Nintendo boasted about its "Mode 7" graphics, which allowed games like F-Zero to offer a greater sense of 3D perspective. Later came the Super FX chip which was added to cartridges to allow games such as *Starfox* and *Stunt Race FX* to use large, solid, fast 3D objects.

SEGA, meanwhile, released numerous add-ons which plugged into the top and bottom of its console. First was the Mega-CD, which allowed games to be released on the new and exciting format of Compact Discs, offering more storage and faster access for games. That was followed in 1994 by the 32X, another plug-in device that doubled the Megadrive's power, and was intended to keep players loyal to SEGA while the next generation of consoles was developed.

In the end though, Nintendo remained victorious, but SEGA had closed the gap. The Super Nintendo sold just over 49 million consoles worldwide, while the Megadrive shifted just over 32 million. Roll on round three!

If you think games are expensive today, remember that some SNES game cartridges cost as much as £70 new. And that was in 1990s money!

MAY THE FORCE BE WITH YOU

Star Wars has inspired dozens of games.
Some were amazing. Others weren't...

Star Wars (Atari)

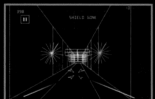

This arcade classic launched in 1983, and put players in the cockpit of Luke's X-Wing battling Imperial TIE Fighters, before swooping into the Death Star trench. Brought to life with crisp vector line graphics, and with voice samples from the movie, this was as close as fans could get to actually being in *Star Wars* thirty years ago!

Super Star Wars

1992 saw the launch of *Super Star Wars* on the SNES. This rock-hard action platformer recreated iconic scenes from the classic 1977 movie, or at least used their locations for relentless shooting and jumping. This is a game in which Luke Skywalker kills the Sarlaac monster in the first level, before slaughtering hundreds of Jawas. Even his battered old Landspeeder comes equipped with plasma death bolts!

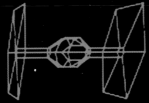

X-Wing

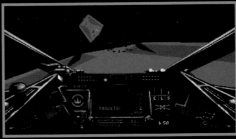

This 1993 PC game took the same level of detail usually applied to serious fighter jet simulations and applied it to the space combat of that galaxy far, far away. A massive hit at the time, it went on to produce multiple sequels, including *TIE Fighter*, which let you play as an Imperial pilot, and inevitably *X-Wing vs TIE Fighter*, a multiplayer classic that let players go head-to-head in these beloved ships.

Masters of Teras Kasi

One of the worst *Star Wars* games ever, this stiff and lumpy 1997 PlayStation beat-em-up pits characters against each other in *Street Fighter*-style bouts. From the ugly 3D graphics to the sheer lunacy of making Han and Luke fight to the death, gamers everywhere had more than a bad feeling about this…

Shadows of the Empire

Before George Lucas got cracking with his universally-loved prequels (stop laughing), it was up to other media to explore stories outside of the original trilogy. The most high profile was *Shadows of the Empire*. It unfolded in comics and this N64 game, which featured mercenary hero Dash Rendar and the evil Prince Xizor.

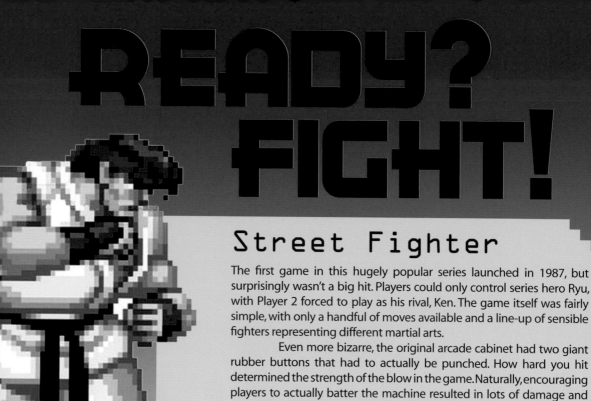

READY? FIGHT!

Street Fighter

The first game in this hugely popular series launched in 1987, but surprisingly wasn't a big hit. Players could only control series hero Ryu, with Player 2 forced to play as his rival, Ken. The game itself was fairly simple, with only a handful of moves available and a line-up of sensible fighters representing different martial arts.

Even more bizarre, the original arcade cabinet had two giant rubber buttons that had to actually be punched. How hard you hit determined the strength of the blow in the game. Naturally, encouraging players to actually batter the machine resulted in lots of damage and the game never really caught on.

That is until the sequel. Out went the novelty controllers and in came a colourful cast of fighters, such as the bestial Blanka, stretchy yoga master Dhalsim and villainous M. Bison. Also new in *Street Fighter II* was the idea of combos; strings of moves that were hard to defend against. These actually happened by accident, as the makers of the game discovered that players were finding ways of fighting that they hadn't planned!

Fireballs in the face! Spines ripped out! Welcome to the golden age of fighting games!

ALTHOUGH fighting games had been around for many years, it wasn't until the early 1990s that the genre really found its groove. With the arrival of 16-bit consoles home gamers could finally experience games that were almost as fast and responsive as those in the arcades, and the prospect of going toe-to-toe with your mates in outlandish martial arts tournaments became a global obsession.

Mortal Kombat

If *Street Fighter II* was the crisp, slick champion of the fighting game scene, *Mortal Kombat* was the snarling punk upstart ready to cross the line in order to make a name for itself.

While the set-up is very similar, with numerous fantastical fighters taking part in a tournament, *Mortal Kombat* certainly didn't shrink from the gruesome reality of what such a contest would actually entail. Its fighters used blades to slice and dice each other, with great spurts of pixel blood pouring forth, while the use of digitised photographs rather than hand-drawn pixel characters made the violence even more confrontational.

If *Mortal Kombat* was famous for anything, it was the Fatality moves. These could be unleashed on a defeated opponent at the end

of a match as they swayed in a stunned state. Memorise and pull off the required series of moves and you could disembowel, decapitate and generally dismember your foe in explicit detail. Little wonder that US politicians got all upset and tried to have the game banned!

SUPER MARIO KART

In which our favourite plumber becomes Nigel Mansell...

IN the early 90s, Mario was forced to shake up his previously comfortable world of platform jumping and reinvent himself as a race driver. Mario himself clearly wasn't built for accelerated stunts, so how could Nintendo possibly compete with Sonic's famous speed? Simple: put him in a car. Or at least a go-kart. And thus, *Super Mario Kart* was born.

When today's games are the subject of dozens of spin-offs and reboots it can be hard to remember just what a seismic shock the launch of *Super Mario Kart* was. Game characters didn't flit between genres in those days. Platformer heroes jumped on platforms. That's what they did. For Mario to suddenly appear in a racing game was borderline anarchy.

Not only that, but *Super Mario Kart* was – and still is – a superb game. It's as much a classic as any of Mario's main series adventures; a perfectly pitched combination of genuine racing game and knockabout multiplayer battle. It's almost unfair. Not only is Mario the undisputed champion of platform games, now he's gone and starred in a brilliant racing game as well. It's like finding out that Robert De Niro is a Michelin-starred chef as well as Oscar-winning actor.

Fun Fact:

The western version of *Super Mario Kart* is censored. In the Japanese original, both Princess Peach and Bowser swig champagne when they win, but Nintendo changed the animation in the US and elsewhere so as not to promote alcohol drinking!

Released in: **1992**

Perhaps what is most impressive about *Super Mario Kart* is how much it feels like a Mario game. For one thing, it was the first game to take Mario's supporting characters and put them in the player's hands. Everyone knew Mario, but being able to take Toad or Bowser for a spin gave them an emotional connection that linear run-and-jump levels never could.

Mario's gold coins become bonus collectables, each one gently increasing your top speed. It's the weapons that most people remember though, in particular those bloomin' shells. A green shell, ping-ponging around a track, is annoying. The red shell, homing in on you as you approach the finish line, is one of the most primal moments of video game excitement and frustration.

Super Mario Kart went on to become one of Nintendo's best loved series, inspiring four console sequels, three hand-held spin-offs and three arcade machines. It also inspired a flood of copycats, with everyone from Pac-Man to The Muppets and even that Crazy Frog thing releasing their own kart racing game over the years!

BIG AND BEEFY
BEAT-EM-UPS!

Cleaning the streets, one roundhouse kick at a time…

JUST as the fighting game genre came into its own, so did its close cousin: the beat-em-up. Don't get the two confused! A fighting game has one-on-one bouts between opponents. Beat-em-ups are the ones clearly inspired by 1980s paranoia over urban crime, where you guide high-kicking cool dude heroes down grungy back streets, kicking and punching dozens of bad guys along the way.

One of the first true beat-em-ups was 1986 classic *Renegade*, which finds you playing as a denim-clad vigilante pulverising your way through street gangs on the trail of your kidnapped girlfriend. Not coincidentally, this was also the plot of pretty much every other beat-em-up that followed. Fun fact: *Renegade*'s original Japanese title translates to "Hot-Blooded Tough Guy". Saucy!

Most famously, and true to most playground sneak attacks that players were familiar with, *Renegade* let you grab enemies by the shoulders and knee them right in the groin. Sadly, there was no way to give the bad guys a Chinese Burn…

Double Dragon

As the name subtly hints, this 1987 game from the makers of *Renegade* let two players deliver fist-based street justice together. Weirdly, butch heroes Billy Lee and Jimmy seem to share the same girlfriend. They're an open-minded lot, these vigilantes.

Final Fight

Capcom got into the action in 1989 with *Final Fight*, a game that distinguished itself by starring Haggar, a topless wrestler with a bushy moustache who was also apparently the city mayor. Why didn't Boris Johnson tackle crime in London by stripping off and bodyslamming a few hoodies? Missed a trick there, Bojo.

Streets of Rage

Released in 1991, this was Sega's attempt to get into the beat-em-up market. Sega understood that such gritty action requires heroes with realistic and relatable names. That's why you play as Axel Stone and Blaze Fielding. Grrr!

TMNT

Konami found a cunning way to jump aboard the beat-em-up bandwagon and stand out from the crowd. It licensed hit TV shows, like *Teenage Mutant Ninja Turtles*, and turned them into multiplayer bash-fests with bright cartoon graphics and audio samples galore. As well as Leonardo and the gang, Konami also made similar games based on the *X-Men* animated series and, bizarrely, *The Simpsons*.

WRESTLEMANIA!

Hulk Hogan and friends made wrestling cool again, and gamers got to grapple along at home!

ONCE upon a time, whenever British people talked about wrestling, they were referring to beefy blokes in leotards like Big Daddy, Giant Haystacks and other literal giants of the UK ring. Matches may have taken place in sports centres and very unglamorous locations such as Wigan, but it was still one of the most popular TV sports of the 1970s and 1980s, with tens of millions of viewers. But as the 1980s drew to a close, there was something else grappling for the audience's affections; something imported over the airwaves thanks to the new-fangled introduction of satellite TV. It was American wrestling, WWF style, and with bombastic stadium presentation and acrobatic gym-chiselled fighters such as Hulk Hogan, Randy Savage and The Ultimate Warrior, it couldn't help but make British wrestling look flabby and cheap in comparison. Naturally, games were quick to seize on this new trend. *WWF Wrestlemania Challenge* hit the NES in 1990, and while it only had a handful of wrestlers with limited moves, it was a massive hit with kids who could now practise body slams without hurling themselves off the top of a bunk bed.

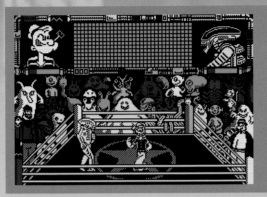

Popeye Vs Alien

Perhaps the most bizarre wrestling game of all time was 1992 effort *Popeye: Wrestle Crazy*. Yes, this grapple-em-up not only starred the bum-faced spinach-loving sailor, but he was also taking part in a galactic wrestling tournament and his first opponent was the xenomorph from *Alien*. It doesn't get much weirder than that!

A flood of officially licensed WWF games swiftly followed, with a parade of seemingly interchangeable names. Can you remember the difference between *WWF Royal Rumble* and *WWF King of the Ring*? Was *WWF European Rampage Tour* really an entirely new game, or was it simply the same game, just with different backgrounds?

It didn't matter! With their neon tights and gaudy face paint, these living action figures were overnight sensations and anything with that glittering golden WWF logo would fly off the shelves faster than Bret Hart off a turnbuckle.

Other games companies tried to muscle in, of course. Capcom released *Saturday Night Slam Masters*, a SNES wrestling game that tried to apply the fighting style of *Final Fight* (and some of its characters) to ring-based bouts, with limited success.

Wrestling was also huge in Japan, which had its own popular wrestlers and game franchises. Indeed, one of these series – 1995's *Toukon Retsuden* – saw the debut of developer Yuke's, who would go on to become the developer of today's official WWE games!

2P OR NOT 2P?

Before the Internet, multiplayer meant sharing a sofa with your opponent!

IT'S taken for granted that these days you can simply fire up your console, select "Join game" and instantly start playing with strangers from around the world. But back in the 90s, when the Internet was still made from rubber bands and sticky tape, if you wanted multiplayer action you actually had to sit next to a real-life friend, and possibly bribe them with crisps. Yes, while today's indie games clamour to bring back the allure of "couch co-op", back in the day that was literally all we had. And it was bloody great.

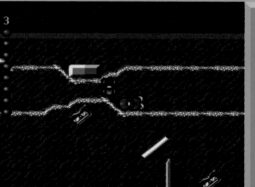

Micro Machines (1991)

The all-time classic local multiplayer racing game! Based on the tiny toy cars, you and up to three friends peg it around miniature tracks on ordinary surfaces like kitchen worktops, school desks and snooker tables. Rather than splitting the screen, the game eliminates the player who gets left behind, ensuring every race becomes a nail-biting battle to keep up with everyone else. Brilliant.

Unirally (1995)

Not many people got to play this oddball stunts-and-jumps SNES racer. That's because a fledgling animation studio called Pixar objected to the cartoon unicycles, which it said were copied from one of its short films, and the publisher was forced to pull the game off sale. Shame, as it's one of the best two-player games ever made.

Sensible Soccer (1992)

Still considered by many to be the greatest football game ever made, *Sensible Soccer* takes its name from the developer – Sensible Software – rather than its often wacky approach to the beautiful game. With its simple pixel graphics and one-button play, this was footy boiled down to its purest form and even people who didn't like the real thing were hooked on this addictive little treat.

Super Bomberman (1993)

Chase your mates around a maze, using bombs to blast open new paths and to catch your opponents off guard. That's the moreish hook of this timeless gem, which uses a constant array of power-ups to keep matches moving quickly. Nothing beats the satisfaction of trapping a mate in between two explosions, just as nothing beats the shame of trapping yourself with your own bombs. Sort it out!

EARTHWORM JIM

The weird and wriggly hero that time forgot!

Released in 1994

MOST 1990s platform game characters disappeared because, frankly, they were rubbish and their games were even worse. That wasn't the case with Earthworm Jim. This was a great character, genuinely funny, and his games were inventive, weird and loads of fun. His origin story is suitably bizarre. An alien spacesuit falls to Earth and is found by a lowly worm. With his head poking out of the top, the self-aware suit acts as his arms and legs as he embarks on a quest to keep the powerful costume out of the hands of scheming villains, as well as rescuing the obligatory princess.

The character was created by comic book artist Doug TenNapel, who was approached by a toy company called Playmates. They'd seen the success of *Sonic the Hedgehog* on the Megadrive and were also producing best-selling toys based on the Ninja Turtles. The plan was to create a character of their own, launching with a game rather than a cartoon series, and then spinning off into lucrative action figures and other collectables.

Marvellous!

Having been created specifically for spin-off products, it's no wonder that Earthworm Jim quickly got his own comic book series – from Marvel Comics, no less – as well as numerous toys and even cool action figures!

Jim even starred in his own animated TV show, which ran for 23 episodes. In the series Jim was voiced by Dan Castellaneta, better known as Homer Simpson himself!

The resulting Megadrive game, developed by Shiny Entertainment with character and level concepts from TenNapel, was utterly bizarre. Not only could Jim use his own body as a whip, but each stage was stuffed with weird gags and slapstick humour. This was a game where you would launch a cow into orbit, bungee jump with a bogie, and face enemies with names like Queen Slug-for-a-Butt and Professor Monkey-For-A-Head. That princess you were supposed to save? She was called Princess What's-Her-Name.

The first game was a big hit, with its lovingly animated cartoon graphics and oddball sense of humour proving popular with critics and gamers alike. A sequel followed in 1995, but there followed a four year gap until *Earthworm Jim 3D* was released for the Nintendo 64. Stiff and ugly, and no longer developed by Shiny, it was a flop and the series never recovered. A HD remake of the cult classic original was released in 2010, but this once-blockbuster franchise has yet to produce another proper sequel. Shame.

GAMES ON TV

The unrepeatable genius of Gamesmaster.

IN the 1980s, if you wanted to know anything about the latest video games, you had to wait for your monthly games magazines to come out. By the 1990s, television was waking up to the potential of this crazy "gaming" fad, and in 1992 Channel 4 gave us the best TV show about games ever made: *Gamesmaster*.

Hosted by sarcastic Scot presenter Dominik Diamond, *Gamesmaster* was an addictive combination of studio banter, reviews, celebrity guests, challenges and wacky stunts. And if that sounds familiar then, yes, *Top Gear* adopted exactly the same format in 2002, swapping games for cars, and became one of the most popular shows on the planet.

Launched at the height of the Nintendo vs SEGA rivalry, and offering the only chance to see the latest games actually being played, *Gamesmaster* immediately became appointment viewing. The fact that Diamond constantly snuck dirty innuendo into the show just made it all the more perfect.

The show's unlikeliest stroke of genius was casting 69-year-old astronomer Patrick Moore as the "Gamesmaster" of the title. With his face distorted by painfully 90s video effects, floating in a weird cyberpunk helmet, he would dispense tips to viewers and introduce games that he clearly knew nothing about. *Gamesmaster* ran for seven series, coming to an end in 1998. There have been many attempts to recreate the show's success, but rivals such as *Bad Influence*, *Bits* and *Games World* just never captured the imagination. Now, of course, you can watch hours and hours of gameplay on YouTube. It's just not the same though…

Top Mag

Gamesmaster spawned its own magazine, which is still going today.

114

Gamesmaster no Moore

Patrick Moore shot his scenes completely separately to the rest of the show. He only met Dominik Diamond once, on the very last day of filming on the final series.

Digitiser

Gamesmaster wasn't the only source of gaming news on TV. There was also the brilliantly daft Digitiser on Ceefax, which combined reviews and news with bizarre characters such as Turner the Worm, The Man's Daddy and a bin-obsessed Mr. T.

Knightmare

Not a show about games but a show clearly inspired by games, 1987 Children's ITV classic *Knightmare* saw teams of schoolkids guiding their blindfolded friend through a computer-generated dungeon, solving puzzles and interacting with actors along the way. The show was famously ruthless. Out of its 112 episodes, only eight teams ever finished the game!

POKÉMON

The best there ever was!

As a child, Satoshi Tajiri loved to go for long walks in the Japanese countryside, looking for insects and cataloguing the ones he found. His friends nicknamed him "Doctor Bug". Later, as a video game obsessed young man, he turned to that childhood love of nature in order to create the game series that would make him a legend: *Pokémon*!

It took him six years to develop the first *Pokémon* games, which were built around the ability to connect two Game Boys together and trade Pokémon between players. That's why every game in the series comes in two editions. *Red* and *Blue* in the first iteration, were both virtually identical, except for a handful of exclusive Pokémon unique to each version.

Whichever game you play, you're guiding a young Pokémon enthusiast as they take their first adventure in the Kanto region, learning how to capture and train Pokémon to take part in battles. Yes, it's a bit weird that this beloved series is based around gladiatorial animal slavery. It's basically cockfighting for kids. Best not to dwell on it too much. Of course, *Pokémon Red* and *Pokémon Blue* were a massive success, in particular because they encouraged players to meet up with friends and make use of the link cable, never one of the Game Boy's most used features. It also meant that lots of people bought two copies of the game, which can't have hurt sales figures!

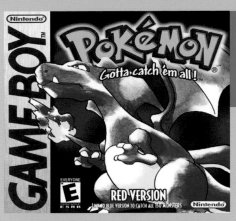

There were just 150 Pokémon in *Red* and *Blue*. Today there are over 800 to find!

The most notoriously rubbish Pokémon is, of course, Magikarp. This useless fish can only flop about and feebly splash at enemies. It's a classic "ugly duckling" though. Put in the effort and it evolves into the powerful Gyarados!

One of the stranger spin-offs is *Pokémon Snap* for the Nintendo 64, a photography simulator in which you travel down fixed pathways, looking for wild Pokémon to photograph.

Record Breaker

Pokémon holds the Guinness World Record for best-selling role playing game series. The core games alone have sold over 200 million copies, and that number jumps to almost 300 million when you add in the various spin-offs!

GAMES GET
SEXY

Or at least they try to, and fail badly…

A large proportion of FMV games sold themselves on the chance to see grainy footage of bad actresses wearing cheap lingerie. With the Internet still a few years away, and its avalanche of free smut still off-limits to all but the most devoted tech nerd, such basic thrills were the best many young men could hope for. But then games had been trying – and failing – to be sexy for quite some time…

Samantha Fox Strip Poker

A perennial bestseller in the 8-bit years, this passable 1986 poker game sauced itself up by offering crudely digitised images of Page 3 "stunna" Samantha Fox in various states of undress. You needed patience to get there though, since she starts the game in a hat, scarf and coat that look like she's leading an Arctic expedition rather than playing a sexy game of cards. Those who did get to view that teasing final image were rewarded with a handful of pixels that could almost be a nipple, if you stood at the other side of the room and squinted a bit.

Sexy Parodius

Trust Japan to show us that being sexy and being weird are not mutually exclusive. *Parodius*, was a series of shoot-em-ups that parodied arcade hits of the time. *Sexy Parodius*, from 1996, was a parody shooter with added bosoms and improbably proportioned Animé girls. Good thing your hands were needed on the joysticks at all times.

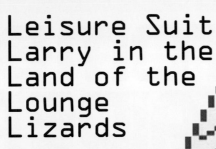

Leisure Suit Larry in the Land of the Lounge Lizards

This 1987 adventure game swapped fantasy forests and wizards for sleazy casinos and motels. Playing as the hapless Larry, you had to get your end away by wooing a parade of different women, almost always ending up humiliated in the process. The games were an odd mix of creaky Catskills club humour, 80s campus comedy sexism and awkward attempts at genuine eroticism.

Cho Aniki

OK, we're deep into the realm of the bizarre now. This infamous 1992 Japanese shooter is populated with dozens of oiled and bulging bodybuilders, in various poses. Understandably adored by cult gaming fans for its kitsch approach, *Cho Aniki* was never meant to be taken seriously – it's an example of a Japanese genre known as Baka-ge, which literally translates to "idiot game"!

TOMB RAIDER

Shorts, pistols, Lucozade and Bono – the wacky rise of a modern gaming icon!

UP until the mid-1990s, the most famous gaming characters were basically cartoons. Despite the eye-wateringly explicit fan artwork you can now find in the darker corners of the Internet, nobody in 1992 fancied Mario or Sonic. That all changed in 1996 when Lara Croft burst onto the scene in *Tomb Raider*.

Part of the first wave of fully 3D polygon action games, along with *Mario 64* and *Quake, Tomb Raider* stood apart thanks to its cinematic vision, its epic scale and – let's be honest – the pert bottom and pointy triangular boobs of its hero.

Yes, a full decade on from *Metroid* and the idea of a female hero was still enough to excite and titillate a sizable number of gamers and games magazines. The reason we played as Lara rather than Larry, however, was rather less interesting. Derby-based developer Core Design figured that the game would look less like an *Indiana Jones* rip-off if the lead character was a woman jumping, climbing and rolling around in dusty ruins than if it was a bloke in khakis.

Of course, it's worth remembering that the first *Tomb Raider* was also a brilliant game. The control and camera feel primitive today, but the combination of environmental puzzles and free-form exploration was downright intoxicating. The moment when – *spoiler alert!* – a hungry T.rex suddenly attacks remains one of gaming's great "wow" moments.

A good game being a success isn't enough to create a phenomenon though, and that's what Lara Croft became. Capturing the post-Britpop swaggering mood, Lara was a legitimate digital celebrity. She advertised Lucozade on TV. She appeared with U2 on a giant screen at stadium concerts. She was on the cover of achingly cool style magazine *The Face*. No chubby plumber or cocky hedgehog had ever broken through into the mainstream like this, and they certainly wouldn't have looked cool and sexy while doing it.

Sadly, as Lara's star rose the quality of her games declined. Under pressure to capitalise on the character's popularity, sequels were hurried into production. The first two follow-ups were still pretty good, and form a solid opening trilogy that fans still love. The games that came after that felt a little more desperate: *Tomb Raider Chronicles* relied on cheesy gimmicks; Lara is presumed dead and the player takes part in flashback missions based on her friend's memories. *Angel of Darkness*, the notorious sixth *Tomb Raider* game was released in a broken state and drove many fans away.

Of course, the character was remade and rebooted in 2013 and is once more back in favour with gamers – even if her global celebrity is no longer quite so in turn with the zeitgeist. Still, it's good to have her around.

Hey, heard about the famous "Nude Cheat" that lets you play the original *Tomb Raider* with Lara in the buff? Well, it's fake. Unofficial PC mods did let mucky-minded fans swap the graphics for geometrically horrifying bosoms and buttocks, but there was never a code hidden in the game. Show some respect!

GAME BOY GREATNESS!

Nintendo's bleeping brick gives us gaming on the go!

AS discussed on pages 20-21, hand-held gaming certainly wasn't new by the early 1990s. There had been dozens of miniature gaming devices in the past, not least Nintendo's own Game & Watch range. The trouble was, none of these were real games consoles – just devices with an LCD screen, like a large digital watch that could only play one thing.

That all changed in 1989, when Nintendo launched the Game Boy in Japan. Designed by Gunpei Yokoi, who had created the Game & Watch phenomenon years before, the Game Boy was an actual games console that fitted into your pocket. Well, if you had pretty big pockets at least.

This chunky delight with its monochrome screen measuring only 160x144 pixels was enough to spark a new wave of gaming mania, as millions of people raced to experience the wonder of games you could play on the bus, at your desk or even on the loo. Freed from the need to be plugged into the telly, new gamers soon experienced the disorienting feeling of putting a game down, only to discover hours had passed. This thing was addictive!

While most consoles were intended to sit under the TV, the Game Boy had to be designed to survive a more rough and tumble life on the move. Shoved into school bags, dropped onto pavements – it had to be able to take a bit of punishment. How much punishment the Game Boy could withstand is shown by this console, owned by a US soldier stationed in Iraq during the 1990 Gulf War. Caught in a bomb blast, and badly burned, the Game Boy may be melted but it still works! The resilient veteran console is on permanent display in the Nintendo World Store in New York for its trouble.

Presidential Gaming

Anyone who was anyone in the early 90s had a Game Boy. Here's Hillary Clinton, chilling out with hers on Air Force One…

Level Up

Nintendo quickly began developing new iterations of its best-selling device, ranging from a smaller pocket model, a version with a built-in light so you didn't need to angle the screen in order to see what was happening, and the Game Boy Color which, as you can probably guess, finally allowed games to be played in colour.

WE'RE DOOMED!

The first-person shooter arrives in all its gory glory.

WHILE there had been first-person games before it was only in the 1990s that PC hardware became powerful enough to really deliver the fast action and complex labyrinths needed to establish the FPS genre for good.

Wolfenstein 3D

The first truly recognisable modern FPS game, this 1992 treat comes from the time when you still had to put 3D at the end of a game's title to let people know it wasn't just a side-scrolling platform game. Deep inside a Nazi castle, it's up to hunky soldier BJ Blazkowicz to gun down the enemies, find the exit and defeat Robot Mecha-Hitler. Based on a true story. Honest.

Doom

The big bad boy of the genre, *Doom* arrived in 1993 and turned gaming on its head. Scary, violent and filled with devilishly designed levels, packed with secrets and bonuses, this was the sensation that ensured first-person shooting would become a gaming obsession for years to come. It was also another blood-soaked early 90s title that led to US Congress considering games censorship. Wimps.

Duke Nukem 3D

The genre's next big leap forward came with this tongue-in-cheek romp, in which macho idiot Duke Nukem saves the world's babes from "alien bastards". Not only could you now explore levels from the air and underwater, but toilets flushed, light switches worked and even pool balls would bounce around the table when shot. It looks crude today, but at the time it was amazing. Also, there were strippers. Just because.

Quake

While previous FPS games had looked 3D, and some even stuck it on the end of their title, most of them used graphical tricks to make you think rooms were on top of each other and flat enemy sprites were moving in 3D space. 1996 sensation *Quake* was the first truly 3D game, made entirely from polygons. The game's bleak industrial aesthetic was backed up by music and sound effects from Trent Reznor of Nine Inch Nails. That's how "late 90s" this game was.

Online goes mainstream

Early FPS games pioneered multiplayer deathmatches, but most were played over local networks or LAN. These were also some of the first games to be downloaded, with players able to get the first third of the game for free, then pay to unlock the rest of the game if they liked it. By the time the first *Quake* demo was released, it was so popular that the Internet itself actually slowed down as millions of people downloaded it at the same time!

BLOCK DROPPING BEATS

The classic puzzle game that emerged from a Cold War research laboratory!

THIS fiendishly-addictive puzzle game was created by Russian developer Alexey Pajitnov in 1984, while working at the Dorodnitsyn Computing Centre of the Soviet Academy of Sciences. Because he was technically working for the Soviet government, and because *Tetris* was originally released by the state-owned software publisher ELORG, Pajitnov didn't receive any money for his creation until he moved to the United States over a decade later, and founded The Tetris Company. Since the game has now sold over 35 million copies, that was probably a very shrewd move!

Like all great games, the rules of *Tetris* are so simple and intuitive that it felt like an old friend, if a little edgy. Shaped blocks fall from the top of the screen and must be arranged to create complete rows, which then vanish leaving space for more blocks. However, the falling blocks are fiendishly-shaped to leave ugly holes in your stack, and if you let the screen fill up then it's game over. It's just like packing your bags at a particularly fast Aldi checkout, basically.

Tetris has one unique claim to fame: it's the only game to have an actual psychological diagnosis named after it! If you ever spent so long on the game that you started to see the falling shapes when you closed your eyes, then you've experienced the Tetris Effect, a genuine term for an affliction suffered by anyone performing a repetitive task so many times that it invades their thoughts and dreams!

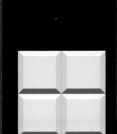

Tetri What?

The correct term for those iconic blocks is Tetriminos!

That famous *Tetris* music is actually a Russian folk tune about a peddler called 'Korobeiniki'. The game was such a phenomenon that it even spawned a Top 40 techno dance remix by the mysterious "Doctor Spin". Who was this mysterious club guru? None other than musical theatre maestro Andrew Lloyd Webber, performing under a fake name!

Block Buster

Believe it or not, a trilogy of science fiction films based on *Tetris* was announced in 2016. Now that's what you call a real blockbuster!

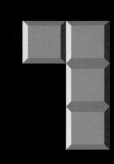

RESIDENT EVIL

Zombies and monsters and madmen… oh my!

THERE had been horror games before *Resident Evil* came along, of course, but it took the power of the new PlayStation console to really put the player inside a creepy, often quite goofy, blood-soaked B-movie.

This Capcom classic gave players two heroes to choose from. Chris Redfield and Jill Valentine are members of the elites S.T.A.R.S task force, despatched to the outskirts of Raccoon City to investigate the mysterious disappearance of another squad. Of course, the other squad has been turned into hamburger meat by the many zombies and mutants created by the Umbrella Corporation, a company so villainous it didn't think twice about using a decaying gothic mansion as the cover for its evil bioweapons laboratory.

The original *Resident Evil* looks a little clunky to modern eyes, with its fixed camera angles and stodgy control system that forces you to rotate Chris and Jill on the spot, and move them backwards and forwards like a tank. Inventory space was deliberately limited, requiring

Resident Evil popularised the style of gaming known as "survival horror", where the emphasis is on staying alive rather than constantly blasting monsters. Needless to say, several other games quickly popped up to explore the same idea.

Clock Tower

This especially creepy Japanese game from 1996 gives you control of several characters, all investigating the mysterious Scissorman killer in Oslo, Norway.

Silent Hill

Konami got into the survival horror genre with this 1999 classic. Surreal and psychological, it finds you investigating the fog-shrouded town as the title in search of your missing child.

constant management of ammo, healing sprays and those ever-present magic herbs, as well as vital items needed to solve the mansion's many puzzles.

In fact, it's a wonder that the Umbrella employees ever got anything done at all, considering that almost every door requires some bizarre combination of statues, medallions, crests and other requirements before it will open and allow you through. Best of all, it was properly scary. If you didn't almost suffer a trouser emergency when those zombie dogs burst through the window, well, you're lying. Down, boy!

Dino Crisis

Capcom capitalised on *Resident Evil*'s success – and the popularity of *Jurassic Park* – with this game, which swapped undead zombies for hungry velociraptors.

WTF FMV!

Full motion video comes to gaming… and ruins everything!

ONCE games started to appear on CD in the mid-90s, developers were granted hundreds of megabytes of storage space. It didn't take long for them to realise this meant they could use actual video clips in their games, and before long we were swamped with dozens of poorly conceived "interactive movies" using Full Motion Video or FMV. With minimal gameplay, low budget special effects and often terrible acting, this was a wave of gaming that definitely deserves to be forgotten…

Night Trap

Certainly the most notorious FMV game of all time, this 1992 interactive horror movie for the SEGA CD gave you control of cameras in a lakeside house full of sorority girls, and tasked you with keeping them safe from vampires known as Augers (though they look a lot like blokes in black pyjamas). The game was laughably tame and absolutely awful, but the voyeuristic nature of the concept put it alongside *Mortal Kombat* on a blacklist of "video game nasties" during the early 90s panic over violence in games. Today, the most sickening thing about *Night Trap* is the quality of the performances.

Phantasmagoria

A point and click adventure played with live actors and computer backgrounds, this super corny horror yarn features a female novelist encountering supernatural peril after moving into the abandoned mansion of a Victorian stage magician who married and killed five women. Unlike *Night Trap*, this game really was incredibly gory and thoroughly deserved its mature rating!

Sewer Shark

Another SEGA CD effort from 1992, this was a very basic shoot-em-up in which you trundled down video footage of monster-infested sewers in an attempt to deliver supplies to human outposts in a post-apocalyptic world. The gameplay involved little more than pointing a cursor at crude enemy sprites while the video background played. Occasionally you'd be interrupted by cheesy characters who barked orders at you, depending on how well you were doing. The actors were terrible, but the SFX were actually pretty good on this one.

Wing Commander 3

Not all FMV games were atrocious. The *Wing Commander* series was already a well regarded space simulator when they decided to use video cut-scenes rather than animation in this 1994 sequel. The acting was pretty good too – Mark Hamill, Luke Skywalker himself, led the cast, with Malcolm McDowell (*A Clockwork Orange*) and John Rhys Davis (*Raiders of the Lost Ark*) supporting him. Creator Chris Roberts went on to direct an actual *Wing Commander* movie in 1999. It was terrible.

...AND MORE NUGGETS!

KILLER GANDHI

A bug hidden in *Civilization 2*'s game code meant that this peaceful spiritual leader's aggression rating went from 1 to 255. This eventually leads Gandhi to threaten other countries with thermonuclear destruction.

LONGEST GAMING SESSION

In 2012, Sydney-based sales manager, Okan Kaya, set a new World Record for the longest ever video game marathon with a whopping 40 hour session. His game of choice: *Call of Duty: Black Ops 2*. His toilet breaks: few, hurried and strained...

SNES SNATCHED

Such was the popularity of the Super Nintendo Entertainment System upon its launch, that consoles actually had to be shipped out in Japan during night hours, for fear of them being stolen by the Yakuza.

ERROR, ERROR

The character of Ermac in *Mortal Kombat* takes his name from the abbreviation of 'Error Macro', which appears in the original arcade game's debug menu. Oh, he's also a psychokinetic ninja composed of dead warrior's souls, don't you know.

SPEAK SIMLISH

Did you know that SimCopter for the PC was actually the first game to feature Simlish, the unique language spoken by *The Sims* characters? It's true. Also, you could fly a helicopter in the game...

OLD MAN KONG

This is such a great bit of video game trivia! Turns out that old Cranky Kong from the Rare *Donkey Kong* games, is in fact the original Donkey Kong from the classic arcade games. Wait, so how come Mario hasn't aged a day in over 30 years then?

WHAT THE FUR?!

Released for the N64 in 2001, Rare's *Conker's Bad Fur Day* is infamous for its greedy, heavy-drinking, foul-mouthed main character. At a time when nearly all N64 games were kid-friendly, Conker's rocked up like a drunken uncle at your birthday.

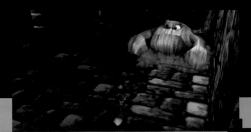

GRAN TURISMO

Put your pedal to the metal with the real driving simulator…

Released in
1997

RACING games have been around pretty much since programmers first learned how to fling pixels on a screen, but for the most part they were simple arcade-style experiences with an emphasis on simple control and thrilling speed.

That changed in 1997 when Sony released *Gran Turismo*, which came with the rather bold subtitle of "the real driving simulator". This was console racing like we'd never seen before, with real cars, properly designed circuits and the best driving physics that PlayStation could muster. This wasn't the sort of game where you could hammer into a bend at full speed and skid your way out of it. You had to think like a real driver, understand the best racing line, and how the back end of the car will react to the things you do at the front. This was a racing game where you had to actually use the brakes!

Naturally, you couldn't just jump into a game like this and start wellying it around whatever track you fancied. This was a game that insisted you took a driving test before taking your place on the grid, and kept requiring tougher and tougher tests to keep taking part in championships.

This demanding approach to a previously fun genre was thanks to series creator Kazunori Yamauchi. He spent five years making the first game, and his perfectionism isn't just the whim of a coding boffin. He was also a dedicated racing driver himself, and since 2009 has divided his time between making *Gran Turismo* video games and actually being a pro race driver in real life!

134

Gran Turismo wasn't the first game to take racing seriously. Here are some of its ancestors…

Indianapolis 500 (1989)

This Amiga game recreated the legendary US endurance race, with 200 real-time laps around the speedway. Of course, most players just wanted to put the impressive crash physics through its paces and muck about with the slow motion action replays…

Revs (1984)

This early BBC Micro racer featured simulated aerodynamics and a serious tone. Creator Geoff Crammond went on to develop classic 3D driving games like *Stunt Car Racer* and *Formula One Grand Prix*.

The Need for Speed (1994)

It's better known today for its fast and furious street racing sequels, but the PC original from way back in 1994 was actually a relatively sober and serious racer with real world sports cars to choose from.

Hard Drivin' (1989)

This famously difficult arcade game boasted an ignition key you had to actually turn to start the game! Realistic car handling in a solid 3D world was balanced against a famous stunt course with ramps and loops for more expert drivers.

TOCA Touring Car Championship (1997)

Gran Turismo's main rival was this British racing sim from Codemasters, which focused on touring car models and UK tracks with realistically drizzly wet weather!

PIXELS AND POPCORN

Super Mario Bros. (1993)

The first ever live action movie based on a game was this notorious turkey, which took Nintendo's bright and breezy colourful classic and turned it into a grungy and violent cyberpunk action thriller. The late great Bob Hoskins starred as Mario, and hated every minute of it, going up against Dennis Hopper as Koopa, a half-reptile supervillain who wants to destroy the Earth. Plagued by production problems, completely missing the joy of the games, and a box office disaster, *Super Mario Bros.* got video game movies off to a catastrophically bad start.

Double Dragon (1994)

This classic two-player beat-em-up certainly had all the ingredients for a cheesy action movie. Set in the futuristic year 2007, it featured martial artist Mark Dacascos and teen TV heartthrob Scott Wolf as battling brothers Jimmy and Billy Lee, pitted against *Terminator 2*'s Robert Patrick, sporting a Jedward-style hairdo as bad guy Koga Shuko. Torn between being a hard-kicking action movie and a kid-friendly romp, the movie was a limp effort and earned just two million dollars at the US box office, going straight to video everywhere else.

Games get turned into movies – and we wish they hadn't bothered!

The 1980s saw several movies that used games to drive their plots. Flicks like *TRON*, *Wargames* and *The Last Starfighter* all acknowledged the allure of these new-fangled entertainments. But they all used fictional games. In the 1990s, Hollywood decided to start taking actual video games and turn their stories into movies. It did not go well…

Street Fighter (1994)

If nothing else, the *Street Fighter* movie was at least an honest attempt to make a genuine video game blockbuster. Jean Claude Van Damme, then at the peak of his fame, starred as Guile, and was joined by Kylie Minogue as Cammy. Together they lead an assault on the villainous M. Bison, played by *Addams Family* star Raul Julia. Almost all the game characters are present, and the film had a couple of good fight scenes. However, fans were annoyed at the changes to the story and critics hated it for being a silly action thriller.

Mortal Kombat (1995)

It's notable that so many of the early video game movies were based on fighting games, no doubt because fighting games had already borrowed their story structure from Bruce Lee's *Enter the Dragon*, with a cackling bad guy running an evil martial arts tournament. That's the set-up for the first *Mortal Kombat* movie as well, which at least understands the goofy comic book tone required. What it didn't have was the extravagant gore of the games, so while characters like Kano and Goro were faithfully recreated on-screen, fans still came away wanting something more.

THE ARRIVAL
OF
PLAYSTATION

A new challenger approaches!

FOR the best part of a decade, the console gaming scene had been neatly divided into a simple binary rivalary: you either backed SEGA or you backed Nintendo. But then in 1995, as a new console generation loomed, the unthinkable happened. A third choice entered the market.

At the time, Sony was best known for its televisions and hi-fi equipment. The idea of a home electronics company like that jumping into the console world seemed bizarre. What did Sony know about games? Quite a lot, it turned out. In fact, if you want to know who to thank for the creation of the PlayStation, turn your attention to none other than… Nintendo. Yes, the console we now know and love as the PlayStation began life as a CD-ROM add-on for the Super Nintendo console. That deal was unceremoniously scrapped and Nintendo started working with rival firm Philips instead. Since we never got a SNES-CD machine, you can guess how badly that decision backfired.

Sony then decided to simply go it alone and release its new-fangled "PlayStation" technology itself. That, of course, turned out rather well…

Sony's console was very nearly named the PSX, after the name PlayStation performed badly in focus group trials.

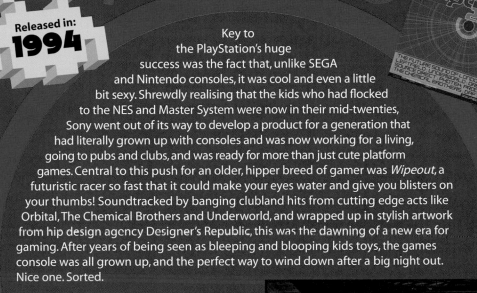

Key to the PlayStation's huge success was the fact that, unlike SEGA and Nintendo consoles, it was cool and even a little bit sexy. Shrewdly realising that the kids who had flocked to the NES and Master System were now in their mid-twenties, Sony went out of its way to develop a product for a generation that had literally grown up with consoles and was now working for a living, going to pubs and clubs, and was ready for more than just cute platform games. Central to this push for an older, hipper breed of gamer was *Wipeout*, a futuristic racer so fast that it could make your eyes water and give you blisters on your thumbs! Soundtracked by banging clubland hits from cutting edge acts like Orbital, The Chemical Brothers and Underworld, and wrapped up in stylish artwork from hip design agency Designer's Republic, this was the dawning of a new era for gaming. After years of being seen as bleeping and blooping kids toys, the games console was all grown up, and the perfect way to wind down after a big night out. Nice one. Sorted.

The original PlayStation, later rebranded the PS One, became the first console in history to sell over 100 million units. The last ones rolled off the production line in March 2005, eleven years after its first launch!

NOT AGAIN!

The dumbest gaming clichés that just won't die!

Glowing Weak Points

Gosh, I wonder how I'm supposed to defeat this enormous boss enemy? Might it have something to do with the conspicuous orange glowing weak spot on their chest? Hmmm. Now explain to me what sort of creature advertises the best way to kill it? Charles Darwin would turn in his grave.

Underwater Levels

These have been a fixture of gaming since the platform games of the 1980s, but it took 3D gaming to make them truly unbearable. Wrestling with the camera while trying to navigate Lara Croft through a tiny underwater gap before she drowns was nobody's idea of fun.

Exploding Barrels

So many evil schemes have come undone because the bad guys never figured out that leaving piles of explosive material in convenient bright red barrels is a really bad idea. And don't get us started on the idiotic henchmen who decide that those barrels are the best place to take cover during a firefight…

Invisible Walls

The early 3D game engines may have been able to show you realistic 3D worlds, but that didn't mean the games were big enough to actually let you explore them. What's the answer? Just stop your character from going any further, even if there's literally nothing in your way. Aarrgh!

Secret Rooms

"Hey, this section of wall seems to be a distinctly different colour to the rest. I wonder what will happen if I shoot it or interact with it? Goodness me, a secret area full of ammo and health! I certainly did not expect that," said nobody ever.

Suspicious Generosity

There you are, low on ammo and desperate for health, when all of a sudden you find a room piled high with bullets, grenades and medkits. Ooh, there's even a rocket launcher. Haven't had one of those yet. This will all be very handy if there's a massive boss fight around the next corner. Oh, there is. What a shock.

Amnesia

Hello there, new gaming hero! Who are you? What's that? You don't remember who you are? And you've forgotten all the useful skills we saw you use in the opening scene? And now we're going to have to spend hours recovering your memories just to learn that you're the Chosen One who will save the world anyway? Oh, go on then…

CRASH BANDICOOT

Wait. The last classic platform gaming hero is a what now?

WHEN the PlayStation launched, Sony's cool new approach may have steered clear of the cute mascots that made SEGA and Nintendo so popular, but they knew that it was never a bad idea to have a beloved character that people associate with your console, just in case.

Enter Californian game developer Naughty Dog, and their pitch for a new kind of platform game that would look and play like an interactive cartoon. Eager to move the action from the traditional side view to a more exciting camera angle that chased the player into the screen, the project was even referred to as the "Sonic's Ass Game" because of the view the player would be getting.

Crash lollops, spins and smashes his way through each level, demolishing crates and hording mango-esque wumpa fruit. Getting to the end of each stage was your immediate goal, but true experts knew that only by finding the secret crystals and opening up hidden routes could you truly claim to have beaten the game properly. Unga bunga!

**Released in:
1996**

Naughty Dog went on to develop the all-action *Uncharted* series for Sony, and even included a scene in 2016's *Uncharted 4* where the player, as hero Nathan Drake, gets to play the first level of *Crash Bandicoot*!

Crash Bandicoot never speaks, as the Naughty Dog team was sick of platform game characters who talked all the time in an attempt to be cool. Here are some of Crash's rivals that may have helped them make that decision…

Gex

This wise-cracking spy-spoofing lizard was best known for his saucy innuendo, which reached its peak – or rock bottom – in his third and final game, 1999's *Deep Cover Gecko*. Co-starring Playboy model Marliece Andrada, it was a weird mix of childish gameplay and smutty humour!

Bubsy

This annoying smart-ass cat starred in a couple of SNES-era platform games, but fell flat on his face on the PlayStation with *Bubsy 3D*, proving to be a game so ugly and so irritating that it's still hailed as one of the worst games of all time.

Croc

Pitched more at younger gamers, this cute baby crocodile only starred in two games of gentle platforming action but was a massive hit with the primary school crowd. In actual fact, the game originally started life as a 3D Yoshi game for the Nintendo 64.

THE RPG GROWS UP

Time for the role playing game to leave its parent's basement and stand on its own two feet...

BY the mid-to-late 90s, and with the advent of the PC as a mature gaming platform, a generation of adult players began looking for experiences with a little more depth, nuance and intrigue.

Ready to meet that need was a little game you may have heard of: *The Elder Scrolls*. This blockbuster series launched all the way back in 1994, but was originally going to focus on first-person gladiator battles. The idea was that in-between a busy day stabbing and slashing in the arena, you would talk to other characters and do jobs for them in order to get better gear for the next fight. Of course, as they added even more characters, stories and sidequests, the arena stuff became less important and the rest, as they say, is history!

As *The Elder Scrolls* began to flesh out its weird and wonderful fantasy realm of Tamriel, it allowed the role playing genre to bust out of the gloomy (and probably stinky) dungeons and castles it had been restricted to by the limited power of earlier hardware, and instead offer a completely open 3D world to explore. You want to be a cat-faced wizard with a sideline in blacksmithery? Go for it!

The Elder Scrolls wasn't the only 90s RPG to make waves…

Jagged Alliance

Released in 1994, this offbeat role player put you in control of a squad of mercenaries on a South Atlantic island that was formerly a nuclear test site. You're there to foil a scheme involving mutant tree sap. Yes, really!

Diablo

One of the first "action RPGs", 1996 hit *Diablo* boiled the RPG down to its thrilling core – mash monsters and grab loot – and opened the genre up to players who preferred a more arcade-style pace.

Fallout

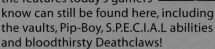

This post-apocalyptic series began back in 1997 with this traditional top-down role playing game. Most of the features today's gamers know can still be found here, including the vaults, Pip-Boy, S.P.E.C.I.A.L abilities and bloodthirsty Deathclaws!

Planescape: Torment

One of the weirdest and most cerebral role playing games ever conceived, this 1999 offering finds you playing as The Nameless One, an immortal being who has forgotten all of their past lives. You must travel through multiple planes of existence in order to learn who you are.

RISE OF THE MMO

Play together, slay together!

IN shifting from table tops to computers, role playing games lost one very important feature: the communal thrill of sharing your adventure with friends. Once computers started connecting together online, the prospect of smashing goblins with your mates was suddenly back in fashion. The earliest efforts were Multi-User Dungeons, or MUDs for short. These text-driven games were played on college and computer lab networks since the 1970s, and so weren't exactly cool. They were fun though, and in 1991 fledgling Internet company America Online decided that offering a multi-user dungeon with graphics would be attractive to a wider audience.

Neverwinter Nights, an official *Dungeons & Dragons* game, debuted on AOL in 1991 and began the process of convincing early web surfers that adventuring with others was a fun fantasy party for everyone, and not the height of anti-social nerdery.

The reason AOL was able to pioneer online play was because all of its users were on its own closed network. To everyone else, the Internet of the early 1990s was still slow and limited, and thanks to a frankly boring and complicated quirk in the way the network evolved, it simply wasn't possible to offer games that connected players together over the open Internet.

That wouldn't change until 1995, when legislation opened up the Internet and games companies rushed in. Within a few years, MUD had morphed into MMORPG, or Massively Multiplayer Online Role Playing Game, and hundreds and even thousands of players could share a virtual world that persisted even when you weren't playing, and evolved alongside its inhabitants. The modern role playing game was here and many never saw daylight again!

Meridian 59

First out of the gate after the Internet floodgates opened was this 1996 game. Players paid a monthly subscription to take part, rather than AOL's costly p████-minute model, allowing them to play all day and all night without going bankrupt!

Ultima Online

Following close behind *Meridian 59* was this 1997 online version of the popular fantasy adventure series. The makers of *Meridian* had tried to popularise the term "MMPRPG" to describe this style of play, but that just sounded like a fart in the bath. Eccentric *Ultima* creator Richard "Lord British" Garriott coined MMORPG instead, and that one stuck!

Everquest

This 1999 Sony game was the first to use a fully 3D graphical style, immersing its players in a fantasy realm of Norrath. Without *Everquest* there would be no *World of Warcraft*, and without *World of Warcraft*, well, we'd have to go outside and who wants that?

THE BEAUTIFUL GAME

How kicking a bit of old leather around led to FIFA mania!

FOOTBALL games have always been hugely popular and have been played by both gamers and fans of the beautiful game alike. Yes, ever since we first learned computers could play games, programmers have tried to make them have a good old kick about.

That's easier said than done, however, when you consider just what's required: ball physics, multiple AI team players all capable of playing a decent match, not to mention a basic level of smoothness and speed. While there were some great footy games over the years, it's understandable that it wasn't until the late 90s that computers and consoles were able to really start doing justice to the sport. That's largely due to EA's *FIFA* series, now firmly established as an annual event, but once upon a time it was just one of many soccer titles jostling for attention.

The series started way back in 1993 on the SNES, but despite having the official FIFA licence, we still had to make do with flat sprites and fake player names. *FIFA '95* introduced club teams. *FIFA '96* added real players and boasted of its revolutionary 3D modelled stadiums. With *FIFA '97* we finally got 3D players instead of sprites.

By the time the whistle blew on *FIFA: Road to World Cup '98*, the series had picked up momentum and was offering the comprehensive fully-featured festival of footy that we know today.

Today, all football games look like *FIFA*, but there have been some other notable standouts over the years…

Peter Shilton's Handball Maradona

Inspired by Diego Maradona's controversial "hand of God" goal in the 1986 World Cup, this 8-bit game from 1986 had you playing as England's goalkeeper, trying to improve your squad by saving goals and encouraging them to play better!

Match Day 2

This 1987 classic was the benchmark for footy games for many years. The technology may have been crude, but code wizard Jon Ritman turned out a superb game of football with incredibly limited resources.

This Is Football

Something of a forgotten classic, this 1999 PlayStation game not only let you take a dive and try to earn a cheeky penalty, it also featured an actual "jumpers for goalposts" mode that simulated a Saturday morning kick about in the park!

Libero Grande

Another Japanese offering, this 1998 PlayStation game had one unique feature: you could play the whole match as the same player, waiting for your AI teammates to pass the ball to you!

International Superstar Soccer

This SNES hit from 1994 was the console footy game of choice for a long time. Based on a Japanese game, where fans are almost as footy mad as the UK, publisher Konami later went on to develop the *Pro Evolution Soccer* series – the closest thing *FIFA* has to a rival!

GOLDENEYE

007 shakes and stirs the first-person shooter.

TODAY, first-person shooters are a huge part of the console gaming scene. The idea of a world where the likes of *Call of Duty* and *Battlefield* aren't topping the charts on PlayStation and Xbox seems bonkers. But it wasn't always this way. Up until the late 90s, the first-person shooter genre was the fiercely guarded territory of PC gamers.

Doom, *Quake* and other FPS classics were designed around the mouse and keyboard, allowing for rapid reactions, the ability to whip your view around in an instant, and swap from shotgun to rocket launcher to quickly blow a lunging hell-demon into bloody chunks. Consoles, with their stubby directional control pads and limited control buttons, didn't stand a chance.

Despite virtually every game based on a movie being utter drivel, the one that made first-person shooting work on consoles wasn't just based on a film, it was based on a James Bond movie: the 1995 series reboot *GoldenEye*, which introduced Pierce Brosnan as 007.

Not only was *GoldenEye* a successful FPS on console, it also managed to be a great James Bond game as well. OK, it didn't quite manage to capture Brosnan's smarmy charms, but it did let you do a lot more than just run around shooting henchmen in the face.

Bond's many gadgets are all present and correct, right down to his high-tech spy watch, so just like the movie character there's always a way out of a sticky situation that doesn't require a speedy trigger finger. You did have to arch your own eyebrow and supply your own terrible puns though.

But still there was more! The Nintendo 64 generously offered four controller ports, and with four joypads plugged in *GoldenEye* offered the first truly indispensable console multiplayer deathmatch. Played in split-screen, with each player using a quarter of the TV, you could choose to play as classic Bond characters and chase each other around.

Okay, so those lumpy-faced sausage people haven't actually aged particularly well, and the game's floaty aiming feels weird compared to today's console shooters, but without *GoldenEye* the FPS genre might never have left the PC. This was one game that left us both shaken and stirred!

GoldenEye also offered some hilarious cheats, including Tiny Bond and Big Head modes. If you're feeling especially brave, try gently lifting the cartridge on one side while the game is running to make all the characters collapse into spasming polygon soup on the floor. Be warned: this can ruin your game forever!

GORE BLIMEY!

We've had some bloody good games over the years. Literally!

AS game graphics became more realistic, and games themselves became powerful enough to allow players to make all kinds of choices, the self-appointed moral guardians began to get more and more manic in their attempts to censor games. Here are some of the iconic moments of bloodshed that got them all hot and bothered!

Death Race

This 1976 arcade game, loosely inspired by the cult movie of the same name, was withdrawn from public use after complaints about the gameplay, in which you had to run over pedestrians to earn points!

Texas Chainsaw Massacre

Yes, there was an official game of the infamous horror movie for the Atari 2600 in 1983! Playing as a blobby blue Leatherface, you had to wander around and kill people with your "chainsaw" – which actually looked like a protruding tummy banana. Despite featuring no blood whatsoever, most US stores didn't risk stocking it.

Dracula

The first game ever to receive a BBFC age rating, this 8-bit text adventure from 1986 was rated 15 because of a handful of pixelated images that were sort of gory, if you stared at them long enough. The game's publisher, CRL, went on to release a Jack the Ripper game that was rated 18, as well as adventures based on Frankenstein and the Wolfman. As well-written as they were, it was hardly the stuff of nightmares!

Splatterhouse

This Japanese arcade hit turned console favourite won favour with youngsters everywhere with its gooey, slimy graphics. Playing as a character that looked an awful lot like *Friday the 13th*'s hockey-masked Jason, you stomped through the levels and squished grotesque enemies with an array of weaponry. Although fairly tame by normal standards, the game was still censored for its Western console release.

Barbarian

This chop-happy 1987 fighting game, inspired by the Conan stories, was notorious for its decapitating finishing move. Land a perfect spinning neck slice and your opponent's bonce would be lopped off instantly. To add insult to an already pretty bad injury, the head was then kicked off screen by a little goblin who dragged the dead body away!

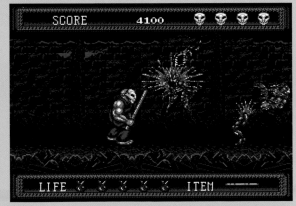

TH CONSOL S THAT COULDN'T

A moment of silence, please…

WE'VE spent many pages looking at the SNESes and Megadrives, PlayStations and Game Boys, but spare a thought for the consoles that were launched into the world – and died on their arse.

3DO

This early 90s flop was unique in one sense: it wasn't just one console. Any manufacturer could licence the hardware rights from The 3DO Company and launch their own version. The idea was to create a single gaming platform, in the sense that different DVD players all play the same discs, but the high prices and muddled concept meant that gamers stayed away. The 3DO vanished from shelves forever after just a few years.

Atari Jaguar

Appropriately, given its name, this console was a bit of a beast. The first true 64-bit games machine, it boasted a couple of genuine classics in its limited library, including the first *Alien vs Predator* game and blistering shoot-em-up *Tempest 2000*. Sadly, it was lumbered with a controller that looks like an early chip and PIN reader, and failed to catch on.

Neo Geo

This one wasn't really a failure, since it was always intended to be a niche device. Developed to use the same hardware and software as SNK's arcade fighting games and shoot-em-ups, players were able to take their cartridges to the arcade and carry on playing there. A nice idea, but once again a high price and limited appeal meant it disappeared quickly.

Philips CDi

Another attempt to create a mainstream home entertainment device that also played games, this was one of the first consoles to run games from compact discs. It was also the only non-Nintendo console to have its own exclusive *Mario* games. Sadly, the games were rubbish, the machine was boring and nobody cared.

Wonderswan

Bandai's attempt to launch a rival to the Game Boy was actually a pretty tasty piece of kit. But it didn't have *Tetris* or *Mario*, and the name sounded like some kind of costumed duck pond crimefighter. Into the bin it went!

VIRTUAL INSANITY

Pop a paracetamol for the headache-inducing world of early gaming VR!

ALL the best games are immersive. They draw you in and make you feel part of their imaginary world. No wonder then, that games developers have been searching for ways to enhance that experience with virtual reality. Today, the likes of Oculus and PlayStation VR mean that functioning, playable VR is a commercial reality on the high street. But that wasn't quite the case in the first flush of VR mania back in the 1990s.

Virtual Boy

Yes, Nintendo got into the VR market early with this infamous 1995 device. You couldn't wear it, so it had to be propped up on a table while you shoved your face into it. Because of the limits of the hardware, all the games were played in dark red and black and many users complained of blinding headaches from staring at these flickering monochrome images up close!

Virtuality

This 1992 arcade system was probably the closest that early gaming got to a recognisable VR experience. Large and heavy, it at least succeeded in putting players inside games such as *Dactyl Nightmare*, *Grid Busters* and *Legend Quest*. Powered by Amiga technology, the downside was the games just weren't very good…

Glasstron

PlayStation VR isn't Sony's first venture into the virtual. Back in 1996 the company unveiled Glasstron, a wearable display apparently designed from *Star Trek* leftovers. This wasn't truly VR though – it simply simulated a giant floating monitor screen in front of you, and was mostly popular with idiot businessmen with more money than sense.

Forte VFX

This 1995 headset at least allowed you to play *Doom* and other first-person shooters in VR. Unfortunately, *Doom* designer John Carmack later described the effect as being like playing the game "looking through toilet paper tubes". He went on to help design the Oculus, so he knows what he's talking about!

The Lawnmower Man

No discussion of 1990s VR would be complete without acknowledging the 1992 movie flop *The Lawnmower Man*. Supposedly based on a Stephen King short story, but actually nothing like it, the film finds Pierce Brosnan's scientist using virtual reality to turn a simple-minded gardener into a digital demigod. The fact that the official game of the movie was a scrolling shooter rather than, you know, an actual VR game pretty much says it all!

GRAND THEFT AUTO

Bad boys, bad boys, whatcha gonna do?

TODAY, the *Grand Theft Auto* name is synonymous with vast detailed 3D cities, enormous budgets and even more enormous sales figures. But it wasn't always this way. Back in 1997, when the series first launched, it was a curious and cartoonish top-down driving game that rewarded you for splatting Hare Krishnas.

Developed by Scottish company DMA Design, who had already had enormous success with *Lemmings*, the game we now know as *GTA* started out under the title *Race n' Chase*, and was inspired more by the frantic maze action of *Pac-Man* than any blood-soaked crime saga. It's fair to say there wasn't a lot to do in the original game, other than drive around doing simple missions and earning points for the mayhem you caused. When that got boring, you could always track down the tank hidden in a corner of the map, and really bump up that "wanted" level!

The main difference with *GTA* was that while previous controversial games had been silly fantasy fare like *Mortal Kombat*, this one actively encouraged you to do naughty things like stealing cars in a supposedly real world setting. At a time when joyriding was causing real world panic, that was all it took to get the tabloid newspapers in a right old lather!

Released in 1997

Notorious tabloid publicist Max Clifford was hired to make sure that *Grand Theft Auto* got the right reputation. He planted stories about the game's content in the media, ensuring parents were up in arms about this fiendish "murder simulator" – which, of course, just made kids want to play it even more!

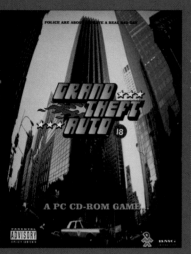

The original *Grand Theft Auto* received an expansion pack set in London in 1969. Inspired by the Michael Caine movie *The Italian Job*, it not only introduced British streets to the game but Mini cars with Union Jack roofs!

The *Grand Theft Auto* game that everyone seems to have forgotten about is 1999 release *GTA2*. Set in the near future, in a city dubbed "Anywhere USA", the game introduced many of the features players now take for granted – such as being able to earn money driving taxis and other vehicles – but its odd science fiction storyline seems to have been quietly erased from the *GTA* canon!

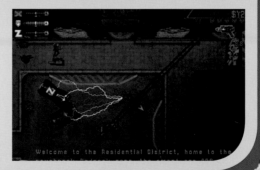

FOR YOUR EYES ONLY

Pay attention, 007! These are the highs and lows
of James Bond's video game career...

```
SHAKEN BUT NOT STIRRED
A James Bond Adventure

You are unexpectedly summoned by
"M", the head of the Secret
Service.
After Miss.Cashcoin has shown
you into the office,"M"outlines
the situation.
A jet fighter has mysteriously
disappeared whilst on a
training mission.
No wreckage has been found but
it is known that the plane was
carrying a nuclear missile
Your task is to locate the
plane and its deadly cargo,and
defuse the missile

Press any key to continue
```

Shaken but not Stirred

007's first gaming mission came in
this almost certainly unofficial 1982
text adventure for the ZX Spectrum.
Summoned to meet with M, you're
given the task of travelling the globe
and putting a stop to the nefarious
schemes of someone called Dr.
Death. Probably not a nice guy.

James Bond 007

A chunky pixel
Bond finally got
to see some arcade
action in this average
self-titled 1983 Atari
game. Rather than adapt
any particular Bond movie,
the game offered four
levels based on action
scenes from *Diamonds
are Forever*, *The Spy
Who Loved Me*, *For
Your Eyes Only* and
Moonraker.

A View to a Kill

The first Bond game to be based on a current movie, this terrible 8-bit adaptation of the 1985 movie features several stages that vaguely resemble scenes from Roger Moore's final turn in the tuxedo. Finish the game and you were treated to the least erotic Bond sex scene of all time!

The Stealth Affair

Bit of a cheeky one, this. The rather excellent 1990 point and click espionage adventure *Operation Stealth* was released in America as an official James Bond game under the new title *The Stealth Affair*. Nobody seemed confused by the fact this British secret agent was now working at the CIA!

James Bond 007

This obscure 1998 Game Boy title features numerous action scenes, as well as gambling mini-games for that authentic casino flourish! Don't forget your bowtie!

007 Action Pack

Not just a game, but a whole computer bundle, this 1990 edition of the ZX Spectrum +2 came with a lightgun and two tenuously Bond themed target shooting games to play with it. Fans were probably more excited by the dossier of fake 007 documents that was also included.

James Bond 007: The Duel

This 1993 Megadrive action game finds Bond shooting and scrolling through the scenery, rescuing attractive ladies and planting bombs. Released four years after *Licence to Kill* hit cinemas, yet still featuring Timothy Dalton's likeness, it is technically the actor's last official appearance as the character!

PARAPPA THE RAPPER

You gotta do what? You gotta believe!

ALTHOUGH dance games were taking off in the late 90s, there was also a wave of music-based games and the biggest hit in that genre was an endearingly odd PlayStation game about a rapping cartoon dog, created by Masaya Matsuura, who both designed the game and composed the songs. The distinctive visual style came courtesy of American artist Rodney Greenblat.

Told entirely through paper-thin characters who flex and wobble through a series of different scenarios, the game tells the story of humble hip-hop pooch Parappa and how he gains the self-confidence to ask Sunny Funny, a sentient flower, out on a date. He does this by learning kung fu from an onion, learning to drive with an angry cow, cooking with a flustered hen and manning a flea market stall with a reggae frog.

Did we mention that this game was super-weird? Because it really was. There's a level where you have to rap to get to the front of the queue for the toilet because Parappa is bursting for a wee. You didn't see that in the Tupac movie.

Gameplay involves tapping the controller buttons in time to the music, which makes Parappa spit his rhymes at the correct rhythm. Hit the beat consistently and his rating goes up to "U rappin' COOL!" Mess it up and you drop down to "U rappin' AWFUL". You must keep your rating high enough to survive the whole song, or else it's game over and Parappa is humiliated.

For those who truly possess mad skillz, yo, there's even the chance to freestyle once you've beaten the game. As long as you stay on the beat, you can replay each stage, ignore the button prompts and remix Parappa's vocals as you go along, triggering a bonus mode in the process.

Parappa was a cult smash, and so inevitably he spawned a sequel and even a spin-off game. In *Um Jammer Lammy*, you played as a sassy female lamb who dreams of being a rock guitarist. Of course.

The success of *Parappa* led to a short but fruitful wave of similar music games. In the minimalist *Vib Ribbon*, you guided a wireframe rabbit along an obstacle course generated from music tracks. You could even put your own CDs into the PlayStation to make levels based on your favourite songs. Other popular "rhythm action" games included *Donkey Konga*, in which you played plastic bongos with Nintendo's famous ape; *Samba De Amigo*, which came with plastic maraca controllers; and *Gitaroo Man*, a bizarre Japanese game about a guitar-wielding superhero!

Released in:
1996

WORLDS WITHOUT FRONTIERS

With great freedom comes great irresponsibility!

Turbo Esprit
This early Spectrum classic featured not one but four three-dimensional cities to drive around, looking out for a gang of nasty drug dealers. With working traffic lights and pedestrians, it was a definite influence on *Grand Theft Auto*.

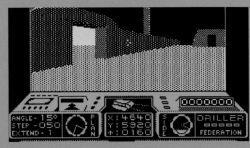

Driller
Another Spectrum hit, this 3D adventure had you drilling holes in a moon to prevent it from exploding. The price players had to pay for this solid 3D world was a frame rate that could be counted in single digits. This game was cool, but painfully sloooow!

Mercenary

Using vector line graphics rather than filled 3D, this great game saw you stranded on an alien world and forced to work for two opposing forces, in order to earn your way off-planet. Unusually for the time, success didn't always mean using violence.

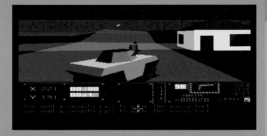

Hunter

Set across a series of islands, this Amiga obscurity was the first free-roaming game to let you take control of whatever vehicle you fancied. From a bicycle to a helicopter, if you could find it, you could take it for a spin!

Midwinter

Still one of the largest games ever made, this action-strategy epic took place on 64,000 square miles of frozen island. Whizzing around in snowmobiles, on skis or even via hang glider, it was up to you how you wanted to lead the resistance against the villainous General Masters!

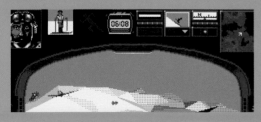

Quarantine

One of the few *Doom*-inspired games to innovate beyond corridors and guns, this game saw you driving a hover-taxi around a post-apocalyptic city, earning fares while gunning down anyone who got in your way. You don't get that these days, not even with Über.

DANCE DANCE REVOLUTION

We like to move it, move it!

IT'S not often that you get to witness the birth of an entirely new genre, but gamers in the late 90s were present for the emergence of the "rhythm game", or as most people think of them "those games where you gimp about on a plastic mat pretending to dance".

Although it really only blossomed with the launch of *Dance Dance Revolution* in 1998, the idea of basing gameplay around keeping a rhythm had been around for a long time. In the early 1970s, Japanese arcade firm Kasco released a game in which you had to lift up girl's skirts in time to music. The less said about that the better, so let's hurry forwards to 1987 when Bandai developed *Dance Aerobics* for the NES.

Designed to work with Nintendo's "Power Pad" – basically a mat with touch sensors that replicated controller inputs – *Dance Aerobics* was part of a series of three family fitness titles, and required players to follow the movements of an on-screen instructor. That was exactly what *Dance Dance Revolution* would offer over ten years later, although Konami took the basic concept and turned it into a sort of techno-era *Saturday Night Fever* dance-off machine, aimed at arcade exhibitionists who thought nothing of prancing about in front of the screen.

Konami dominated this niche sub-genre, even going so far as to set up its own music game development department called Bemani. Other games to emerge from Konami's rhythm game obsession were *GuitarFreaks* (which saw you playing a fake guitar), *DrumMania* (which had a fake drum kit) and *BeatMania* (which let you play at being a club DJ). All of these games, of course, would be instrumental – pun very much intended – in inspiring the wave of plastic instrument music games in the 2000s, such as *Guitar Hero*, *DJ Hero* and *Rock Band*.

Dance Dance Revolution was a massive hit in the West as well as in Japan, and other companies quickly rushed out their own dancing games, all of which sounded like depressing provincial club nights with names such as *Pump It Up*, *In The Groove* and *MC Groovz Dance Craze*. There was a dancing game based on Disney's *The Jungle Book*, and even a Christian version called *Dance Praise* with uplifting gospel songs to bop along to!

The result was not only a wave of copycat games, but hundreds of cheaply-made dance mat controllers. To this day, no high street charity shop is complete without a tatty unbranded PlayStation dance mat slowly losing its colour in the window…

SNAKE

Games? On mobile phones? It'll never catch on…

SMARTPHONES have become such an integral part of daily life that it can be hard to remember that they're a very recent invention. It wasn't so long ago that a mobile phone was exactly that: a phone that you could put in your pocket. If you were lucky it had a small green screen large enough to show a few lines of text, or maybe a crude picture. And if you were very, very lucky it was a Nokia 6110 and you could play *Snake* while waiting for the bus.

Perfectly designed to fit into the 240x320 screen of this early handset, *Snake* starts out as more of a stubby worm. Destined to continually slither forwards, you must flip left and right at 90 degrees in order to avoid hitting the edge of the screen. Points were earned by eating the little blobs of food, but each one also made your tail grow longer. Very soon, the challenge is not avoiding the walls but not crashing into yourself as you coil around the screen.

If *Snake* was unusually addictive, it's because the game was already technically 20 years old by the time Nokia literally put it in the palm of our hand. The first sighting of this classic game was way back in 1976, in the arcade game *Blockade*, in which two players shared the screen and had to trick or trap the other. And if that sounds familiar then, yes, the same idea was "borrowed" for the arena in 1982 gaming movie classic *Tron*.

There's a reason so many 90's kids now look back on these crude early phones with so much fondness. While gaming hardware everywhere else had moved on by leaps and bounds, for the PlayStation generation the Nokia 6110 was a glimpse back into the very dawn of gaming, with its tiny memory and limited pixels. The lesson that even a few dots shuffling around a tiny space could be utterly absorbing was a useful one, as gaming in general thundered towards the 21st century.

It's notable that very few other games managed to make a splash on these phones. *Tetris* was included on some devices, but since games could only be built-in as permanent features rather than downloaded and added to these early handsets, there wasn't much demand to make new games for them. The irony, of course, is that today members of that "Millenial" generation use their state of the art iPhones to download and play accurate emulations of that original Nokia *Snake* game. Nostalgia always gets you in the end!

Released in:
1997

THE END OF AN ERA

The SEGA Dreamcast paved the way for the modern games console…
and paid the price for being first!

THOSE who were born after the year 2000 have always known Sega as the company that keeps making *Sonic the Hedgehog* games, publishes *Football Manager* and occasionally puts out re-releases of old retro games. Pity them, for they did not know Sega at its height – they have never known SEGA, the console manufacturer.

By 1998, SEGA's once proud console legacy was, to be frank, in a pretty shabby state. Megadrive owners had been milked with half-baked add-ons like the 32X and Mega-CD, and the follow-up console, the SEGA Saturn, came and went almost without being noticed. The SEGA Dreamcast, the company's next console, would also be its last.

And that's the real tragedy here because the Dreamcast was a gorgeous bit of kit! This sleek white box of delights was a beefy little thing, boasting a bunch of exclusive games that were both stylish and fun. From the dayglo skate mania of *Jet Set Radio*, the sun-kissed driving mayhem of *Crazy Taxi*, the multiplayer fighting madness of *PowerStone* to the highly camp dancing of *Space Channel 5*, this was the SEGA fans remembered from the 80s: bright, colourful and shamelessly entertaining, godammit!

The Dreamcast had more to offer than just cool games though. It was the first console to boast loads of features we now take for granted. It was the first modern console to offer online access as standard, with a built-in modem. With *Phantasy Star Online* it was home to the first console MMORPG. It was even, technically speaking, the first console to have HD graphics as standard. It seemed to have everything a gamer could want, but the Dreamcast also faced a lot of hurdles. Its piracy protection was ridiculously easy to crack, meaning anyone with a CD burner could copy games. Stung by the poor performance of the Saturn, large publishers like EA decided not to release their games for the Dreamcast. Worse, just as the Dreamcast launched, Sony announced the PlayStation 2 and millions of gamers opted to save up for that instead.

Despite pioneering so many of the features that still drive today's console games, the Dreamcast was discontinued in 2001, only a few years after launch and, with that, SEGA hung up their console producing boots. It was the last gasp of the classic era of gaming, but in its failure the Dreamcast also paved the way for how we play today, ushering in the concept of the modern games console. Not a bad legacy, all things considered…

SHENMUE

Looking for sailors in a chilled-out revenge saga!

AS gaming ticked over into the 2000s, designers began to get even more ambitious in the sort of experiences they wanted to create. One such designer was Yu Suzuki, creator of arcade classics like *Space Harrier* and *Out Run*, who hungered to tell stories that were both more epic, and also more human.

He got his chance when SEGA abandoned plans for an adventure game based on the *Virtua Fighter* series, with that project morphing into *Shenmue*, a weird mixture of gentle slice-of-life drama set in a small Japanese town and martial arts revenge thriller.

Taking place in 1986, you play as Ryo Hazuki, a young man trying to discover who killed his father. While his quest does involve some chases and fights, for the most part you advance the story by wandering around the town, driving forklift trucks, asking where you can find some sailors, and looking after a kitten. Most people will remember it for the even more random activities available, such as collecting Sega toys from vending machines, and enjoying fully playable versions of classic Yu Suzuki arcade games.

Time passes, seasons change, things even get festive at Christmas time, and it's easy to forget you're supposed to be avenging your poor murdered dad. Can't we just stay here and chill?

Released in:
1999

SEAMAN

Scientifically proven to be the most disturbing game ever!

MANY games have tried to conjure up an artificial intelligence worth having a conversation with, but few did it quite as horrifyingly as *Seaman*.

There's no easy way to explain it: this is a virtual pet game in which you talk to a fish with a human face. And, yes, that's literally all you do. Using the Dreamcast's microphone attachment, you must chat to the hideous abomination to find out how to take care of him. This, despite the fact that any right-thinking person would happily leave him to starve and run screaming in the opposite direction.

Eventually, the aim is to nurture and – god help us – breed Seaman until he evolves into an amphibious frog creature. At which point he is able to leave the water and, presumably, lead his species in attacking and devouring the souls of humanity.

If that wasn't weird enough, the western release of the game was narrated by Leonard Nimoy, Mr. Spock himself!

Face it!

Seaman's human face is actually Yutaka "Yoot" Saito, the game's designer!

Released in:
1999

GAME OVER
CHECKLIST!

Tick off any of the games you've played to see if you're a true retro geek!

- 007 Action Pack
- 1942
- A View to a Kill
- After Burner
- Air Raid
- Alex Kidd in Shinobi World
- Alien Vs Predator
- Alien-8
- Angel of Darkness
- Art of Fighting 2
- Astro Wars
- Atic Atac
- Auf Wiedersehn Pet
- Automania
- Back to Skool
- Banjo Kazooie
- Barbarian
- Battlefield
- Battleships
- BeatMania
- Beneath a Steel Sky
- Blockade
- Broken Sword
- Bubbler
- Bubsy 3D
- Call of Duty
- Castlevania
- Castlevania II: Simon's Quest
- Castlevania III
- Cho Aniki
- Civilization
- Clock Tower

- Crash Bandicoot
- Crazy Frog
- Crazy Taxi
- Crossy Road
- Dactyl Nightmare
- Daley Thompson's Decathalon
- Dance Aerobics
- Dance Dance Revolution
- Dance Praise
- Death Race
- Deep Cover Gecko
- Diablo
- Dig Dug
- Dino Crisis
- DJ Hero
- Dog's Life
- Donkey Kong
- Donkey Konga
- Doom
- Double Dragon
- Dracula
- Driller
- Drive Time
- DrumMania
- Duck Hunt
- Duke Nukem 3D
- Dungeons and Dragons
- E.T. The Extra Terrestrial
- Earthworm Jim
- Earthworm Jim 3D
- Elite
- Elite: Dangerous
- Everquest

- Everyone's a Wally
- Excitebike
- Fallout
- FIFA '95
- FIFA '96
- FIFA '97
- FIFA: Road to World Cup '98
- Final Fantasy
- Final Fight
- Football Manager
- Forest of Doom
- Frankenstein
- Frankie Goes to Hollywood
- Futuridium EP
- Ghostbusters
- Ghosts 'n' Goblins
- Gitaroo Man
- GoldenEye
- Gran Turismo
- Grand Theft Auto
- Grid Busters
- GTA2
- Guitar Hero
- Guitar Freaks
- Gunfright
- Gyromite
- Hang-On
- Hard Drivin'
- Herbert's Dummy Run
- Horace and the Spiders
- Horace Goes Skiing
- Hungry Horace

- Hunter
- Hyper Sentinel
- In The Groove
- Indianapolis 500
- International Karate+
- International Superstar Soccer
- Jack the Ripper
- Jagged Alliance
- James Bond 007
- James Bond 007: The Duel
- Jet Pac
- Jet Set Radio
- Jet Set Willy
- Killer Instinct
- King's Quest V
- Knight Lore
- Legend Quest
- Leisure Suit Larry in the Land of Lounge Lizards
- Lemmings
- Lemmings Paintball
- Libero Grande
- Licence to Kill
- Little Computer People
- Lone Wolf
- Maniac Mansion
- Manic Miner
- Mario Bros.
- Masters of Teras Kasi
- Match Day 2
- MC Groovz Dance Craze
- Mega-lo-mania
- Mercenary

- Meridian 59
- Metroid
- Micro Machines
- Midwinter
- Mindwheel
- Miner Willy Meets the Taxman
- Mortal Kombat
- Mrs Mopp
- Neverwinter Nights
- Night Trap
- Out Run
- Pac-Man
- Paperboy
- Peter Shilton's Handball Maradona
- Phantasmagoria
- Pitfall
- Planescape: Torment
- Pokémon
- Pokémon Snap
- Popeye: Wrestle Crazy
- Populous
- Porky's
- Pro Wrestling
- Pssst
- Pump It Up
- Pyjamarama
- Quake
- Quarantine
- R-Type
- Rebel Planet
- Renegade
- Resident Evil
- Revs
- Rock Band
- Sabre Wulf

- Sabrina
- Sam and Max Hit the Road
- Samantha Fox Strip Poker
- Samba De Amigo
- Saturday Night Slam Masters
- Seaman
- Seas of Blood
- Sensible Soccer
- Sewer Shark
- Sexy Parodius
- Shadows of the Empire
- Shaken but not Stirred: A James Bond Adventure
- Shenmue
- Silent Hill
- Sim City
- Sim Earth
- Skool Daze
- Snake
- Sonic the Hedgehog
- Space Channel 5
- Space Harrier
- Space Invaders
- Space Quest
- Spacewar
- Splatterhouse
- Stack up
- Star Trek
- Star Wars
- Starring Charlie Chaplin
- Stop the Express
- Street Fighter
- Street Fighter II
- Streets of Rage
- Super Bomberman
- Super Mario Kart

- Super Smash Bros.
- Super Star Wars
- Symphony of the Night
- Tapper
- Tempest 2000
- Tetris
- Texas Chainsaw Massacre
- The Adventures of Lomax
- The Biz
- The Comet Game
- The Elder Scrolls: Arena
- The Hobbit
- The Incredible Hulk
- The Jungle Book
- The Last Ninja
- The Lawnmower Man
- The Muncher
- The Muppets
- The Need for Speed
- The Perils of Willy
- The Rats
- The Secret of Monkey Island
- The Shaky Game
- The Simpsons
- The Stealth Affair
- The Thompson Twins
- The Wolfman
- This is Football
- Three Weeks in Paradise
- Tic Tac Toe
- TIE Fighter
- TMNT
- Tomb Raider
- Tomb Raider Chronicles
- TOCA Touring Car Championship

- Track & Field
- Tranz-Am
- Trashman
- TRON
- Turbo Esprit
- Ultima Online
- Um Jammer Lammy
- Unirally
- Uridium
- Vampire Killer
- Vib Ribbon
- Virtua Fighter
- Warlock of Firetop Mountain
- Way of the Tiger
- Weetabix versus The Titchies
- Wham: The Music Box
- Wing Commander 3
- Wipeout
- Wolfenstein 3D
- World of Warcraft
- Worms
- WWF European Rampage Tour
- WWF Royal Rumble
- WWF Wrestlemania Challenge
- WWR King of the Ring
- X-Men
- X-Wing
- X-Wing Vs. TIE Fighter
- Xevious
- Zero Wing

How did you score?

- 1-65: Impressive Gamer
- 66-132: Hardcore Gamer
- 133-200: Gaming Geek
- 201-269: Gaming God!

STUDIO PRESS BOOKS

First published in the UK in 2017 by Studio Press Books,
an imprint of Kings Road Publishing, part of Bonnier Books UK,
The Plaza, 535 King's Road, London, SW10 0SZ
www.studiopressbooks.co.uk
www.bonnierbooks.co.uk

978-1-78741-095-4

Written by Dan Whitehead
Edited by Kirsty Walters
Designed by Grant Kempter for Cloud King Creative

Printed in Turkey

While every effort has been made to credit all contributors, Studio Press would like to apologise
should there have been any omissions or errors, and would be pleased to make any
appropriate corrections for future editions of this book.

Picture Credits

With special thanks to Paul Baxter.